PATH
REBORN

Starting a New Job

BALD SOLOMON

PATH
SERIES™

CHAPTER ONE

It was the very first day on the job—but never too soon to put out fires.

Lydia Boaz pulled into the bustling parking lot of New York Meat's headquarters, her blood coursing with excitement. As a divorcee, she'd had to collect the fragments of her broken marriage and carefully mold them into a new life. It had taken her some time, but she had finally done it, by working hard and remembering to stay positive. After graduating college and landing a new job, things were finally coming together.

The building that towered over the parking lot was an impressive sight. Made of glossy granite, it glistened in the sun like crystal. Its tall, slender windows reached several stories into the sky, giving off a sense of grandeur. In front of the building was a majestic set of marble stairs that led up to an intricate brass door handle shaped like an eagle with its wings outstretched. The door was made from thick mahogany wood, polished with gold-colored hinges and arched handles.

As Lydia walked through the entrance, she felt like she had entered another world filled with splendor and luxury. The lobby had high ceilings adorned with intricate chandeliers dripping with crystals that glittered brilliantly in every corner. Large marble columns lined up against one wall and supported a balcony at the top floor where Lydia could see plush velvet curtains hanging down.

Today was her first day as Chief Financial Officer of the massive meat processing company, New York Meat. Lydia straightened her blazer and adjusted the purple shawl around her neck. She was ready to embrace this new chapter. *Here it is, the first day of the rest of my new life.*

As she entered the front lobby, people hurried past with stacks of paperwork and rolled dollies loaded with boxes. The energy electrified her.

"Hey, Lydia!" A tall man with graying black hair extended his hand.

Lydia remembered him from her panel interview. Grant, the plant manager.

"Hey, Grant," Lydia said warmly. "Good to see you again."

"You too! We're thrilled to have you on board."

Lydia smiled broadly. "It's wonderful to be here. I'm eager to dive in."

Grant gestured for her to follow him. "Let me give you a quick tour and take you to meet with the CEO."

Lydia's heels clicked on the tile floors as she followed Grant through the maze of cubicles and offices. First, he showed her to her office, and then he gave her a tour of the departments she'd be working closely with. The rapid pace and constant movement invigorated her. She had worked hard to reach this executive position, and she would do whatever it took to make her mark and prove herself.

As Grant pointed out the various departments and described the operations, Lydia's mind spun with ideas. She was ready to streamline processes and improve the bottom line. This was her time to shine.

Grant's expression turned serious as they approached the CEO's office. "Before the official introductions, I need to discuss something with you. We've had back-to-back fires at some of our facilities across the state over the past few weeks. While it's possible it could've been from machinery overheating or grease catching fire, there's also a chance that it's arson."

Unease washed over Lydia like a wave as she contemplated the implications of such events. She had only heard rumors of the fires, but now that she was close to them, it felt even scarier. Her skin crawled with anxiety as she thought of how these acts of destruction could damage the company's reputation and, of course, increase costs.

She clenched her jaw, trying to suppress the fear that was slowly creeping up inside her belly. She knew this was not something to be taken lightly. If anything happened on her watch, it would reflect poorly on her and could potentially jeopardize her new position.

Her thoughts raced in different directions as she considered all the variables at play: *Could there be an internal issue? Was it a disgruntled employee or customer? What measures could they take to prevent future incidents?*

Lydia needed to stay calm and focused to help protect New York Meat from further damage or danger.

But it wasn't just protecting the company that concerned her; the idea that an arsonist could be lurking about frightening her. It reminded Lydia of another dark time in her life.

"Lydia?" Grant's voice pierced through her thoughts. "A-Are you okay?"

Lydia perked up, nervous and embarrassed as she realized how long she'd been quiet. "Oh, yes. Sorry, just trying to memorize where all these departments are."

"Yeah, it's a pretty big place," said Grant, nodding.

"It certainly is," Lydia replied. "And arson? That's terrible."

Grant nodded grimly. "The police and fire investigators are on it, but there's been little progress. It's got everybody on edge."

The knot in Lydia's gut tied tighter. This was an unexpected crisis to handle so early on.

Grant stopped walking and put his hand on her shoulder reassuringly. "We realize it's a bit unconventional for you, as the CFO, to investigate these fires, but nearly everyone in management has had a go at this, and we've got nothing. Our Rico thinks maybe we're all too close to it, and we're missing something. He thinks you coming in with fresh eyes might make a difference."

Lydia straightened her posture. This wasn't something she wanted to take on so soon, but she had to look confident.

Stay positive, Lydia.

Staying positive was one of the critical factors in helping Lydia rebuild her life after her divorce from Abe, and she wondered how it might help her in this situation as well. *In what ways can a positive attitude ease my transition into this new environment?*

"I'll do what I can to help," she said firmly.

Grant smiled and reached for the door of the CEO's office. "Rico's expecting us," he said as he pulled the door open.

Lydia was stunned by the grandeur of the mahogany and marble-covered space, dripping with crystals that glittered brilliantly in every corner.

A large wooden desk with intricate carvings dominated the room, with a leather-backed chair facing it. Seated there was an older man, white-bearded and wearing a black suit, his piercing eyes trained on them as they entered the room. He gave them a curt nod before addressing her directly, and Grant waved goodbye to them both before turning and leaving the room.

"Welcome, Lydia. I am glad to have you on board." His voice was firm and authoritative, with a surprising warmth in it that put her at ease. "It is my pleasure to meet you in person." He gestured for her to approach his desk.

Lydia approached the desk, extended a hand, and introduced herself.

"Rico Lane," said the CEO with a firm handshake. "We have a situation that I am sure Grant has briefed you on. I need your help investigating these two fires that have plagued us lately. Obviously, the authorities will do their own investigation, and we will cooperate with them completely. But I'd also like to do an inside, sort of informal company investigation. Our shareholders always get a little anxious when incidents like this happen that cause us to lose money, and they'll be on my back about it. Being proactive and conducting our company investigation will show them how invested we are in preserving and earning back our company profits as well as demonstrate our overall accountability." Rico paused and took a swig from the glass of water on his desk. He placed the glass down gently, looking thoughtful. "A few of us here have taken a crack at it, but we didn't get far. We'd like to get some fresh eyes on it."

Lydia already felt the pressure of the task, but if she could successfully tackle this issue for the company, she could prove her value.

Rico shook his head. "I wonder what could be behind these fires. Accidents? A competitor who wants to sabotage us? An employee we laid off in the past?" He brought a fist under his chin and squinted. "Did you know fame, or even, revenge, are some of the key reasons people commit arson?"

"No, I didn't," said Lydia. "That's very interesting."

He then went into detail about the locations of the two targeted facilities and described the destruction created by each blaze. Lydia listened attentively as she wrote down her observations and questions.

When he finished his explanation, Rico fixed her with an intense gaze. "Lydia, I need you to go to the most recent location and find out what you can," he said firmly. "I will provide additional resources to help your investigation."

Lydia nodded, her dark hair swaying across her shoulders. She thanked him for his trust in her. She was both excited and anxious about uncovering the truth behind these mysterious fires, and she was determined to do her best. She walked out of Rico's office, ready to get started on this vital mission.

When Lydia arrived at the charred remains of the Central Warehouse, she coughed against the lingering smoke. Firefighters and police officers swarmed the area, and Lydia's eyes watered as she took in the destruction.

As she walked toward the rubble, Lydia felt her foot kick something across the sidewalk, and she looked down to see a plastic item skittering over the pavement. As she looked closer, it appeared to be some sort of pipe. *Interesting. What's this?*

She bent down and picked it up before walking closer to the arson site.

"Sorry, ma'am," a police officer said to Lydia, motioning her away from the scene. "You can't be here."

"I'm the CFO of New York Meat," said Lydia. "This is one of our—"

"Doesn't matter, ma'am," the officer interrupted.

"She's with me," said someone behind her.

Lydia turned to see a man in a firefighter's jacket surveying the scene. His keen eyes were fixed on the plastic item in her hand. "Lucky B, State Arson Investigator," he said, flashing a badge.

The officer squinted at the badge, and then nodded grimly.

"You must be Lydia," said Lucky with an easy smile, extending a hand. "Rico said you'd be coming down."

"That's right. Lydia Boaz, CFO of New York Meat," she responded. She shook his hand firmly.

"Your CEO seems to think this might be the work of an arsonist—and they might be one of your own," said Lucky. "He called me personally and told me he sent you here to talk to me. What do you think?"

What do I think? It's my first day on the job. "Well, I haven't been at the company very long. I can't say I have any leads. You have any ideas?"

Lucky gestured around the ruins. "Well, there are only a few ways fires usually start in a plant like this: equipment malfunction, which usually happens when a machine runs too long and overheats. Then there's poor wiring within the building, but that's much less common. There's oil—if someone spills it and it catches fire. But all three of those would cause the fire to start on the inside. Based on the burn patterns and incendiary evidence, this fire started outside the building, just like the other recent fires. So not only was it not an accident, but it was also likely done by the same person."

Lydia's jaw clenched. "Well, Lucky, it seems we have a common goal in finding the culprit. I look forward to working with you on this investigation."

Lucky smiled. "Definitely. It's great to have someone on the inside. Just let me know if you come across anything."

He glanced meaningfully at the item in Lydia's hand, but to Lydia's surprise, he didn't ask her what it was.

With that, he turned and strode away, leaving Lydia alone amid the wreckage. She looked down at the pipe-shaped item, gears turning in her mind. Was there more to this fire than met the eye?

Lydia felt a surge of anxiety shoot through her as she contemplated the magnitude of the situation. She had expected to investigate questionable accounting practices or uncover cases of fraud, but this was something entirely different. This was no longer about finding discrepancies on paper—it was now about tracking down a dangerous individual who intended to cause serious harm. Her chest tightened.

How could she possibly find out who caused this fire? What if they were never caught?

She suddenly felt overwhelmed by the enormity of her task, and disappointment settled in. Was she really up for this challenge? She had been so eager to prove herself when Rico had asked for her help, but now she couldn't shake the feeling that maybe this wasn't what she had in mind after all. Clearing her mind, Lydia steeled herself and pushed aside her doubts.

She tucked the pipe in her bag and headed back to work, mind racing. In the privacy of her office, she examined the item more carefully. It was wider at one end, with a screw-on attachment piece to fasten it to something else. It was slightly curved and tapered to a small opening at the opposite end. It was a nozzle—

Is this...a gas can nozzle?

She lifted the item to her nose and breathed in slowly, the unmistakable smell of gasoline registering in her brain. *I have to tell someone!*

Lydia decided she'd contact Lucky B soon to tell him what she'd found, but for now, she had to get some work done.

She placed the curiosity in the bottom drawer of her desk, staring at the drawer thoughtfully long after she had closed it. Then she glanced around her office, her eyes settling on the calendar on her desk. As she examined it, she noticed she had a meeting with the board of directors scheduled on Friday to discuss the fires.

So soon?

She had less than a week to prepare an update about the fires to the board. The very thought was intimidating, but this was her chance to take charge of the situation and prove herself as CFO.

Well, I better get started.

LYDIA STRODE INTO the executive boardroom with determination, taking her seat at the head of the table.

"Ladies and gentlemen," she began, choosing to be confident despite her nervousness. "I recently met with Arson Investigator Lucky B, who has confirmed that the fires were deliberate."

A murmur ran around the table as the gravity of the situation hit home. Lydia continued confidently. "Mr. B is investigating to identify the perpetrator and neutralize any further threats."

The board members looked at each other nervously, unsure what to do next. Lydia felt a stab of fear in her chest. She knew they were relying on her to lead them through this challenging situation, but in truth, she had no idea what to do either. Inhaling deeply, she forced herself to stay calm and speak firmly.

But more than being firm, she wanted to be warm and encouraging. Acknowledging that she was a new face to all of them, it was important for Lydia to make sure all their interactions were friendly and uplifting. *How can I maintain positivity in all my workplace communications?*

Lydia paused, and she smiled broadly as she looked around the room.

"But I've done my research on all of you," she said, still smiling. "And you guys are the best in the business. So we're going to be okay." She noticed smiles and a few nodding heads at this compliment. So she continued. "The best thing we can do is to cooperate fully with the arson investigator. Let's figure out how we can best support Mr. B's investigation and ensure our safety moving forward."

The board members quickly agreed, and Lydia felt a rush of relief. As they discussed the situation, she felt a spark of hope that this case would be resolved soon.

She stepped out into the warm evening air when the meeting ended, feeling more optimistic. She was about to turn away when something caught her eye—standing at the edge of the sidewalk was Lucky B, arms crossed and looking like he was waiting for someone. When their eyes met, he gave a slight nod and began walking toward her.

"Ms. Boaz," he said when he reached her side. "I thought we might have another quick chat. I was wondering if you found anything important at the scene—besides that plastic pipe I saw you with."

"Oh, yeah!" said Lydia, remembering the nozzle she had found. She had been so busy with work, it had nearly slipped her mind. "That! Okay, this might sound crazy but—I actually think it's a gas can nozzle!"

Lucky B perked up noticeably, his eyes clear and wide. "Really? Do you still have it? I'll need to turn it over to the police."

"Yeah, definitely," said Lydia. "Hang here for a second, and I'll go grab it."

Lydia went up to her office to retrieve the nozzle. She gave it to Lucky B, still wondering why he hadn't asked about it when she'd first found it.

Lucky took the item and examined it thoughtfully. "I can't imagine you've dealt with a situation like this before," he said, finally looking up.

"No, I haven't. But I'll manage. Is it all right to start coordinating cleanup and repairs?"

"Sure," said Luck B. "We have everything we need from the scene."

"Great," said Lydia. "Thanks a lot. I better get to it."

The following Monday, Lydia met with Rico again. As they discussed the arson case, Lydia told him about her visit to the arson site and what she had seen.

Rico looked dejected as she spoke, his chin in his palms. She hesitated before finally asking him what was wrong. His face softened as he answered her question.

"Another one of our warehouses has been burned," he said quietly. "I'm afraid it's the third one this month."

Lydia paused before responding. *Things are getting bad quickly.* Too quickly for me to even do anything.

Lydia felt the memories of a frightening past spread like dark shadows through her mind. She'd had her own experience of a nefarious person lurking in the shadows…watching, hiding, always just out of sight. An icy fear gripped her chest, its bone-chilling tendrils constricting her. She would never forget that haunting time.

"What do you need me to do?" she asked him firmly, wondering if she shouldn't have.

Rico shook his head. "Lydia, you don't have to take this on. It's gotten worse than I imagined it would. We have a Chief Operating Officer, Diego, who can spearhead the investigation if you want him to. You just started with the company, and it's not fair for us to ask you to be responsible for something so critical this quickly."

Lydia could feel her anxiety dissipating as she listened to Rico's words. She felt energized by his trust in her and was more than willing to let Diego lead the investigation while she focused on rebuilding their warehouses.

"Thank you for understanding," she said sincerely before rising from her seat and giving Rico a firm handshake.

"I do believe Diego has meetings all morning, though," said Rico. "Why don't you just go check out this latest fire? You can pass the details along to Diego later on."

"Sounds good," said Lydia with a nod, and she left the office and made her way out to the latest arson site.

Lydia arrived at the east side Nod Warehouse, and her stomach dropped at the sight of it. Not again.

The building was partially burned, its walls blackened and charred from the blaze that had swept through it that morning. Firefighters and policemen swarmed the area, scurrying about the perimeter of the still-smoldering building.

The windows were shattered, and a few doors had been burned down in the fire's wake. Water pooled on the floor, and scattered pieces of machinery lay strewn across it.

The smell of smoke was heavy in the air, mixing with another scent Lydia couldn't quite put her finger on––a combination of burnt plastic and metal, which made her nose wrinkle in disgust.

Further inspection revealed that only one side of the facility had been damaged by fire; the other appeared untouched.

Lydia's heart sank at the destruction. Months of lost production. Hundreds of thousands in damage.

She turned to find someone approaching from behind her, and she was happy to see that it was Lucky B. He walked up and greeted her.

"Care to take a look around with me?" he asked with an easy smile.

"Oh, definitely," said Lydia, grateful to have this opportunity to work with a professional.

As Lucky began his inspection, Lydia wandered the perimeter, looking for clues. And she spotted something—a partially burned business card wedged under a fallen beam. She pulled it out carefully.

Lucky's head snapped up. "What do you have there?"

Lydia examined the singed card. Half of it had been burned away, but she could make out part of a name. Her blood ran cold. "It's one of our employee's cards. Mitchell Irving. But…he works with me at the office."

Lucky raised an eyebrow. "Is there a reason his card shouldn't be here?"

"Well, he works in marketing," Lydia explained. "Over at the office building. He really wouldn't have an occasion to be here, nor would the laborers here at this plant have any need for his business card."

Lucky B was staring at her intently.

Lydia met his gaze, resolve steeling her nerves. The game just got personal.

"Perhaps I have a traitor in my midst."

CHAPTER TWO

Delilah Boaz stepped out of the taxi and gazed up at the towering skyscrapers, the honking horns and bustling crowds overwhelming her senses. This was it. New York City. Home to her mother Lydia. The place of her dreams, ripe with opportunity and adventure.

Here goes the next chapter of my life.

She hauled her overstuffed suitcase up the stairs to her new apartment, excited as ever. Unlocking the door, she scanned the modest studio, envisioning how she'd make it her own. As she gazed at the boxes that seemed ubiquitous in the empty apartment, she sighed in relief, knowing her mother was coming over soon to help her unpack.

Delilah opened the first box, stowing her clothes and hanging photos on the walls. She smiled wistfully at a picture of her and Jobe on a hiking trip, remembering their laughter and playful banter. Her smile faded as, moments later, emptying her suitcase, she uncovered a letter from ex-boyfriend Jude, his familiar scrawl addressing her so formally—Delilah Boaz. He had given it to her back in Alexandria when they had decided to take a break, and in it, he'd poured out his heart, saying there would always be a place for her in his life. She wondered if keeping it made it more difficult for her to move on.

Even now, thousands of miles away, without Jude nearby, without her lifelong soulmate Jobe Johnson nearby, it seemed she couldn't avoid thinking about both of them.

She sighed, the familiar pang of indecision hitting her. Would pieces of her old life always follow her?

The doorbell rang, and Delilah shuffled to the door and let her mother in.

Delilah wrapped her in a hug. "Hey, Mom!"

"Hey, darling," said Lydia, squeezing Delilah tightly. Then she looked around the apartment. "Oh, Delilah, I love this! You get so much natural light!"

Delilah grinned. "Isn't it great?"

"Yes, honey!" said Lydia, still looking around. She had wandered into the bathroom, and Delilah could hear the sink faucet running. "And good water pressure!"

Delilah laughed. Her mother was always going on about water pressure.

"Nothing worse than taking a shower with low water pressure," Lydia was saying when she came back into sight. "You know?"

Delilah laughed again. "Yeah, Mom. I know."

"Well, let's get to it," said Lydia, grabbing a stack of plates from one of the boxes and carrying them into the kitchen.

"So, how's the new job, Mom?" said Delilah.

Delilah saw a falter in her mother's step, and her mother was quiet for a moment.

"It's good, honey. I'm really getting the hang of things."

Delilah set down the box she was carrying. She knew something was wrong. "What's wrong, Mom?"

Lydia shook her head as she placed a mug in the cupboard. "It's nothing, honey."

Delilah walked over to Lydia. "Mom, talk to me."

Lydia turned and met her gaze, a look of worry clouding her eyes. "Well, you know those fires…"

"Yeah, what about them?" Delilah asked.

"The company's been targeted by an arsonist and— they've asked me to investigate."

Delilah's eyes shot wide. "You? Investigate? Why?"

"It's a bit unconventional," said Lydia with a faint shake of her head. "But New York Meat has decided to do an informal company investigation alongside the one law enforcement is doing. A show of good faith to the company's investors, and a way to get a fresh pair of eyes on it."

Delilah took a deep breath and exhaled slowly. "That sounds stressful. You've just started this position."

Lydia shrugged. "Definitely not what I expected. But that's not what really bothers me. It's the fact that… there's an arsonist out there who's targeted us. And it could be anyone—someone I work with and talk to every day. It just…it feels like twelve years ago all over again. I know it's not the same but…"

Delilah shuddered just thinking about what her mother had endured all those years ago. The fact that someone had—

"I don't want you to worry about it," said Lydia. "I mean it, honey. Everything will be fine."

Delilah took her mother's hands in her own. "I know, Mom. And you're going to rock this investigation!"

Lydia smiled. "You think so?"

Delilah squeezed Lydia's hands excitedly. "Oh, definitely! This is so crazy—you're like a detective now? Do you have any leads, Detective Boaz?"

"Oh, stop it," said Lydia, laughing.

"I'm serious!" Delilah exclaimed. "Or is it classified information?"

"Well," said Lydia in a playful tone. "No one has told me I can't share details about the investigation."

"Yes!" Delilah screamed playfully. "Tell me, tell me, tell me!"

Lydia looked Delilah in the eyes. "I'll tell you everything—just as soon as I have something to tell."

"What?" said Delilah, her shoulders slumping in disappointment. "Well, that was anticlimactic."

"Sorry I couldn't be more entertaining. But I've got nothing so far."

"Well, I guess you've only just started," said Delilah with a sigh.

"Yeah, exactly. Give me a break."

They continued unpacking for the next several hours, until the setting sun covered the city in dim orange light. Lydia went home, and Delilah prepared herself for a work event she'd be attending in the next few hours.

Delilah gazed out the window overlooking the chaotic streets below. Yellow taxis vied for space between honking sedans and delivery trucks. People crowded the sidewalks, walking with purpose. The city teemed with energy and possibility.

She was starting a brand-new job as the Communications Lead for the New York Association of Meat Producers, and landing the position had been an enormous accomplishment. Now all she needed to do was prove to herself that she was up for the challenge. This was it, she reminded herself—a new chapter. She would throw herself into this job, into building connections and starting over. This time, she'd choose her own direction.

Delilah took her platinum blonde hair out of a ponytail and combed it. Then she braided the vibrant tresses into two pigtails and picked out clothes for later. Tonight was the company happy hour, her first chance to meet some of her new coworkers.

But first, she wanted to write. She'd bought a new journal in anticipation of this moment. Its deep blue cover was smooth against her fingertips, and the blank white pages felt like a promise. She opened it to the first page and felt the weight of every word she would write here—all that this journal could become. She wrote the first line: "It is my first night in New York City. The very beginning of my new life."

DELILAH STEPPED INTO the humid evening air, at once enveloped by the sights and sounds of the city. Sirens wailed in the distance as crowds jostled along the sidewalks. The aroma of hot pretzels and coffee blended with car exhaust and cigarette smoke. This was nothing like her sleepy hometown.

Weaving through huddled groups, Delilah made her way toward a trendy rooftop bar, the location for the work happy hour. She rode the elevator up, nerves fluttering in her stomach. Stepping out onto the sleek, modern rooftop patio, Delilah scanned the animated crowd. Clusters of sharply dressed professionals laughed and mingled, drinks in hand. The Manhattan skyline glittered around them.

A friendly-looking brunette was waving at her. "Are you here with the 'Namp?'" the woman asked playfully.

Delilah nodded and smiled. "The 'Namp'? Oh my gosh, I love that!"

"Yeah, because who wants to say the New York Association of Meat Producers every time?" the young woman explained.

"It's definitely a mouthful." Delilah laughed.

"And who wants to spell out the acronym, N.A.M.P? So, it's like, 'Namp!'" The woman laughed, and Delilah laughed right along with her.

"I'm Delilah." Delilah extended a hand.

The woman shook Delilah's hand excitedly. "I'm Jenia."

Delilah looked around at the bustling rooftop. "This place is incredible."

"It's not a bad view, right?" Jenia grinned and flipped her dark hair away from her eyes. "Let me introduce you around."

As Jenia led her from group to group, Delilah worked to match names and faces, making small talk. The team seemed educated and driven, if a bit pretentious. She noticed sidelong glances at her casual sundress and flats.

Finally, a slim man with horn-rimmed glasses waved them over. "Jenia, aren't you going to introduce me to our new recruit?" He turned to Delilah, extending a hand. "Tyler Hunt. A pleasure."

"Delilah Boaz," she replied, shaking his hand. Something about his shark-like smile made her uneasy.

"Delilah here is going to be working on the new marketing campaign," Jenia explained.

Tyler raised an eyebrow. "Is that so? How fortuitous." He leaned in, voice lowered. "A bit of advice? Don't trust a word Clarissa says. Her promises don't mean much."

Delilah blinked, surprised. "Clarissa?"

"Our illustrious leader," Tyler muttered, adjusting his glasses.

Jenia shot him a look. "I'm sure Delilah will form her own impressions." She touched Delilah's arm. "Why don't we freshen up our drinks?"

Delilah followed Jenia to the bar, Tyler's cryptic warning echoing in her mind. What had she gotten herself into?

Jenia handed Delilah a glass of wine. "Don't look so worried. Tyler likes to stir up drama."

"So there's no issue with Clarissa?"

Jenia hesitated. "Well, Clarissa can be…difficult. But she's brilliant, and if you stay on her good side, you'll go far here."

Delilah nodded slowly. She'd dealt with tough bosses before.

"Anyway, enough shop talk," Jenia said brightly. "Are you seeing anyone? Leave a trail of broken hearts back home?"

Delilah laughed. "Not exactly." She thought of Jobe's kind eyes, Jude's intoxicating smile. "It's complicated."

"Isn't it always?" Jenia winked.

They chatted easily about life in the city, favorite foods, and weekend plans. Despite Tyler's warning, Delilah felt herself relaxing.

As the party wound down, Delilah gazed out at the glittering skyline. The future spread before her, filled with challenge and possibility. Taking it all in, she turned to join her colleagues, ready to take the first steps toward whatever lay ahead.

ON MONDAY, DELILAH entered the sleek office building, smoothing her blouse and adjusting the bag on her shoulder. Today was her first day of work. The lobby was all polished stone and gleaming metal, with stylish furniture and modern light fixtures. Delilah crossed the cavernous space, heels clicking on the floor, and she entered the elevator.

As the elevator ascended, Delilah's stomach fluttered with anticipation. What would her new job be like? Would she fit in with her coworkers? She thought of the networking event, Jenia's friendliness, and Tyler's warning about their boss.

The elevator dinged, the doors sliding open. Delilah stepped out onto the bustling floor. People rushed past carrying files and cups of coffee. Delilah wound through the maze of cubicles until she found a door marked "Clarissa Klein: Editor-in-Chief." She took a steadying breath and knocked.

"Come in." The voice was crisp and no-nonsense.

Delilah entered. Behind a sleek glass desk sat a woman with short curly hair, wearing smart black frames and an emerald blouse. She examined Delilah coolly.

"You must be Delilah. Have a seat."

Delilah sat, clutching her bag.

"I'll keep this short, as we have work to do." Clarissa shuffled some papers on her desk. "While you come highly recommended, this is the big leagues. I expect nothing short of excellence from my team."

Her gaze was piercing, and Delilah resisted the urge to shrink back into her chair. Clarissa briefed her on her first project—an exciting marketing campaign—and while Delilah was certainly picking up on a no-nonsense vibe, Clarissa ended the briefing with a warm smile that was almost enough to put Delilah at ease.

"Give me your best, and you'll be rewarded. Fall short, and you'll be gone before you know it." Clarissa checked her watch. "I'm needed in a meeting. My assistant will show you your desk."

She whisked out the door, leaving Delilah reeling. She took a shaky breath, Tyler's warning ringing in her ears.

This job would test her limits, that much was clear. But Delilah never backed down from a challenge. She stood, smoothed her blouse once more, and stepped out to find her desk.

The real work was just beginning.

She followed Clarissa's assistant, a mousy young woman named Alice, through the bustling office space. Desks and cubicles were filled with people reviewing documents and notes, or rushing between stations clutching papers and coffee mugs.

At last, Alice gestured to a small office with a desk along the back wall. "Here you are, Delilah. Let me know if you need anything." She hurried off before Delilah could respond.

With a sigh, Delilah sat and looked around, glancing around at her coworkers. Most were fully engrossed in their work, but a few shot curious looks her way.

One man caught her eye and smiled friendly, and she noticed it was Tyler from the party. As soon as he finished scribbling a note, he wheeled his chair over.

"There's the newbie," he said, offering his hand.

Delilah shook it with a smile. "Long time no see, Tyler."

"I know, right?" Tyler leaned back in his chair. "Don't let Clarissa scare you off. She acts tough, but deep down, she's a big softie." He winked.

Delilah laughed. "Good to know. This is all a bit overwhelming, but I'm excited for the challenge."

"You'll do great. We're happy to have you on the team." Tyler checked his watch. "I've got a meeting soon, but let's grab lunch later. I can give you the inside scoop on how things work around here."

"I'd love that, thanks." Delilah waved as Tyler wheeled back to his desk, feeling a bit less adrift.

Delilah pondered Tyler's offer. She was grateful to have found a friendly face so quickly. But she wondered about his motives—was he genuinely trying to help, or aiming to gossip and stir up drama? She would have to continue cautiously until she had him figured out. But she knew it was important to speak openly and regularly with coworkers. *I wonder how often I should check in with Tyler?*

It was an important question, but for now, she had work to do.

Delilah's pen flew across her notebook as she wrote up ideas for her first project. The office hummed with activity around her, but she tuned it all out, focusing intensely on the task at hand.

This first assignment would set the tone for her career here. She had to nail it. The stakes felt high, but it was a thrill rather than a burden. Delilah lived for this kind of pressure. It sharpened her mind and brought out her best work.

After an hour, she leaned back to review what she'd written. Not bad for a start. Her brain felt pleasantly tired, like a muscle after a good workout.

A knock at her office door made her jump. She looked up to see Tyler leaning against the entrance.

"Hey! How's the first day going?" he asked.

"Good so far; I just finished up some initial brainstorming. What's up?"

Tyler glanced around before stepping inside. "Well, I just wanted to give you a heads-up about something." He lowered his voice. "I've heard Clarissa is already gunning for you."

CHAPTER THREE

Lydia's boots crunched through the charred remains, sending puffs of ash into the air. The pungent smell of smoke lingered despite the days that had passed since the fire. She scanned the ruins, taking in the collapsed beams, melted pipes, and mounds of debris. This was the first of the two facilities hit by arson, the Central Warehouse, and curiosity had drawn Lydia back to the scene.

Although Rico had given Lydia permission to pass this investigation off to Diego, their COO—and Lydia certainly intended to—she felt the least she could do was give Diego as much information as possible before she handed off the daunting task.

Kneeling, she examined a partial footprint pressed into the ashes that stood out to her. The pattern was unlike any print she had ever seen—dozens of little circles overlapping each other. *That might be important.* Lydia filed away the details.

The thought of a stalker lurking in the shadows filled her with dread. Twelve years ago, after her divorce, a man had stalked her, and she had never been more afraid in her life. She had no desire to be involved in any more situations involving dangerous individuals.

Her mind flashed back to those months when she would wake up in the night to strange noises outside her window or see a figure in the distance before it melted away into darkness.

But the footprint intrigued her. She decided to take a chance; maybe the second site would have more evidence. She shouldered her backpack and headed out of the ash-filled wasteland.

The light was fading as Lydia arrived at the second arson site, Nod Warehouse. Here, the damage wasn't as extensive. Only one side of the building was burned. She moved past fallen beams, charred debris, and broken glass scattered across the floor.

But there in the ashes was another set of prints matching the first.

Lydia paused, conflicted. While the prints might have been a vital clue, she reminded herself that she didn't want to get involved. Stepping into this mystery meant uncertainty and danger.

Lydia returned home, the image of the prints with the circles etched in her mind. Delilah would visit tonight, and Lydia hoped her daughter's warmth and wisdom could settle her swirling thoughts. She had a decision to make, but for now, she took comfort in knowing Delilah was on her way.

Lydia took a moment to be grateful that her daughter now lived in the same city as her, just fifteen minutes away.

"I'm so happy Delilah has moved here to New York!" Lydia thought out loud. But even amid these positive thoughts, the gravity of the arson weighed heavily upon her.

Lydia sat on her living room couch, staring absently out the window. She thought of the shoe prints at both arson sites, identical in their strange tread.

But did she want to get further involved in the investigation?

Just then, there was a knock at the door, and Lydia knew it was her daughter. She opened the front door, and Delilah breezed in.

"Long time, no see!" Delilah joked, embracing Lydia warmly.

Delilah's smile and energy lifted Lydia's spirits instantly. She was grateful for her daughter's visit during this stressful time.

"How are you holding up with everything?" Delilah asked gently as she sat down.

Lydia sighed. "I just don't know if I should get involved in finding who did this," she admitted. "It could be dangerous, and the police are already looking into it."

Delilah nodded sympathetically and squeezed her mother's hand. "It's so scary. Whatever you decide, I'm here for you."

Lydia felt a swell of gratitude for her daughter's unconditional support. The visit had lifted a weight from her shoulders.

"You know, Michelle is visiting next week," Delilah said. "You should talk to her—she always has such good advice."

Lydia nodded, remembering the guidance that Delilah's best friend, Michelle, had offered Delilah in the past. Though free-spirited, Michelle had a knack for seeing situations clearly.

"In fact, when I was hesitating about helping Dad save the meat plant back home, Michelle really put things in perspective," Delilah continued.

Lydia recalled Delilah's uncertainty about getting involved in that crisis. It had been a big step for her daughter.

"Having someone like Michelle to confide in means so much," Delilah said warmly. "It reminds me of how Jobe was there for people during the flood several months ago."

Lydia nodded. She had heard that Jobe had grown into a leader during that disaster. Stepping up during that extreme time had shaped him profoundly.

"Yes, you are probably right. Grandpa Mosie always used to tell us that the true essence of life lies in your impact on those around you. Maybe this is …" Lydia's voice trailed off in thought.

Perhaps investigating the arson could be a similar turning point for her, Lydia considered. But the anonymous threats troubled her deeply.

Delilah squeezed Lydia's hand again. "I'm here for you, no matter what," she said gently. "We'll get through this."

Lydia managed a small smile, comforted by her daughter's steady presence. The path forward remained unclear, but Delilah's support gave her strength for the challenges ahead.

Lydia cleared her throat, gathering her thoughts. "Speaking of Jobe," she said, "tell me more about how he stepped up during the flood."

Delilah nodded, a bittersweet look passing over her face. "Well, he had just lost his job, and even though everyone wanted him to look after the town—especially with his firefighter background—he didn't want to take it on. She paused and smiled, no doubt picturing Jobe's calm determination amid the chaos. "But he stepped up anyway. He coordinated the emergency response. He got people to safety, secured buildings, gathered supplies, and led the sandbag distribution. His leadership held the town together."

Lydia listened intently, imagining the young man's courage.

"In the end, his efforts saved countless homes. The town survived, largely thanks to him." Delilah shook her head in admiration. "That experience changed him. Gave him confidence and purpose."

She looked at her mother meaningfully. "It's definitely scary, Mom. But…I know you could do it. I mean, if you want to."

"Well, I love the confidence you have in me," Lydia said with a little laugh. "I just…I don't know. Maybe I have PTSD or something from that stalker years ago."

"Oh, Mom!" said Delilah with a dramatic frown. She leaped forward and wrapped Lydia in a hug. "Don't worry. Arsonists just like to burn things for attention. It's not personal, you know. Has nothing to do with you personally."

Lydia relished her daughter's embrace, and they rocked back and forth for a few moments before letting go.

"You're right, honey," said Lydia. "This is totally different."

Delilah nodded in understanding. "It's still scary. But just remember, no one's after you—they're after your buildings."

Lydia smiled and nodded heartily. "That's a good way to look at it."

"And who knows," said Delilah with a shrug. "Maybe tackling this challenge will lead to some sort of transformation, just like it did with Jobe."

Lydia winked at her daughter. "You never know.

After a thoughtful pause, Lydia's expression lightened. "You know, I never understood why you and Jobe didn't become a thing. He's so perfect for you!"

Delilah laughed softly. "Oh, Mom, you're biased. You've always loved Jobe. Jobe is a wonderful person, but I just don't know if anything more was meant for us."

Lydia grinned and shook her head. "I think you just don't see what I see, dear."

The two women sat in comfortable silence, taking solace in each other's company.

DELILAH ENTERED THE crowded ballroom, trying to calm her nerves. It had been three weeks since she had started her new job, and she was attending the annual business mixer for the New York Association of Meat Producers.

Spotting the bar, she made her way through the mingling guests. After ordering a glass of wine, she scanned the room, hoping to find a familiar face.

"Delilah! There you are!" someone exclaimed behind her.

She turned to see her co-worker, Priya, waving her over to where she stood with Jenia and Tyler. Relief flooded through her.

Delilah went over to them. "Hey, guys."

"Hey, girl!" said Jenia.

"Glad you could make it," said Tyler, adjusting his glasses.

"I'm so glad you're here too," said Delilah as she joined them. "I was afraid I'd be wandering around alone all night."

"Not a chance!" said Priya, putting a friendly hand on her shoulder.

Delilah felt herself relaxing, and the group chatted amiably about their work and lives outside the office. She found herself laughing along with them, the conversation flowing easily.

Over the next hour, Delilah circulated the room with Priya and Jenia, meeting other colleagues and board members. She felt increasingly at ease, chatting and joking with those around her.

By the end of the evening, Delilah realized she had made more connections in one night than in her entire three weeks on the job. Her earlier trepidation had vanished.

As she said goodnight to the friends she had made, Delilah marveled at how quickly her world had expanded. Stepping outside her comfort zone had been worth it. She reflected on just how much more confident she felt in her new role having connected with her colleagues, and she realized connecting and communicating was essential to succeed at a new job. And she pondered: *What else could I do to create some new friends?*

The following morning, Delilah arrived at the office energized and eager to get to work. The mixer had ignited her motivation.

She began tackling projects, researching leads, and brainstorming fresh approaches. The hours flew by in a blur of productivity.

Around mid-afternoon, her supervisor Clarissa stopped by Delilah's desk. "I just wanted to say how impressed I am with your work today," she said. "You've gotten further ahead than I expected on the marketing campaign."

Delilah smiled, thankful for the acknowledgment. "I'm excited about this project. I think it has the potential to really expand our reach."

Clarissa nodded. "I agree. Why don't we meet first thing tomorrow to discuss strategy? I'd love to hear your ideas so far."

"That would be great," said Delilah. As Clarissa walked away, Delilah felt a surge of satisfaction. She had proven herself, and had gone above and beyond expectations.

It made her wonder about Tyler's warning: *I've heard Clarissa is already gunning for you.* It sure didn't seem like it after such praise. Sure, Clarissa was a no-nonsense, tough-love sort of boss, but she hadn't done anything to cause Delilah to be concerned. She wondered if instead Tyler was the troublesome one.

Though Delilah hasn't yet seen an issue with Clarissa, she is curious about her own performance thus far. She wondered if it met Clarissa's standards, and if not, how she could remedy that. *What should I do to make sure I do the top-quality work that Clarissa expects?*

Delilah had asked herself when she had first started who she could turn to for guidance, and she initially thought that person might be Tyler, since he had offered. But considering his divisive nature, she felt it might be better to look toward coworkers like Priya or Jenia if she needed help.

She spent the last hour of the day working diligently, trying to get as much done as possible. When it was time to leave, she stopped by Clarissa's office.

"Do you have a few minutes? I'd love any feedback you have on my work today."

Clarissa gestured her in. As they reviewed the project, she provided praise along with some constructive criticism.

Delilah took the critiques seriously, making notes on how she could improve. More than anything, she was grateful that Clarissa took the time to nurture her growth.

As Delilah headed home, she marveled at her success in expanding her business network and connecting with new colleagues, as well as her initiative in asking Clarissa about her performance and getting the answers she needed. She'd come far in just a short time. With renewed confidence, she couldn't wait to see what tomorrow would bring.

LYDIA SAT ALONE in her living room, curtains drawn against the dark night outside. The ticking of the grandfather clock marked the passing minutes as she stared absently ahead.

She couldn't stop thinking about the arson sites she had visited, the charred rubble and lingering smell of smoke haunting her thoughts. While part of her was desperate to uncover the truth, another part resisted getting involved. What if pursuing this puts her or her loved ones at risk?

But this was an arsonist, Lydia reminded herself. They targeted buildings, not people.

Lydia sighed, shifting restlessly on the sofa. She was just starting a new path in life. Was it worth jeopardizing everything she had worked for?

At the same time, the image of those distinct shoe prints kept flashing through her mind, luring her to uncover whatever significance it might hold.

Lydia remembered that Delilah was coming by, and she would've left the door unlocked for her, but…she was afraid.

Minutes later, upon hearing knocking, she went to the door and looked through the peephole. Her daughter stood outside the door.

Lydia unlocked the door and opened it.

"Hey, Mom!" Delilah called.

Lydia perked up happily as Delilah came in. Delilah's presence soothed her rattled nerves. They exchanged a warm hug before sitting down.

"Rough day?" asked Delilah.

Lydia nodded. "I can't stop thinking about those arson cases. She sighed. "I just don't know what to do."

They continued talking late into the night, Delilah encouraging her mother to speak with Michelle soon. The visit would come at the perfect time.

Lydia sent Delilah off with a big hug.

She arrived at the office early the next morning, and she sighed softly as she settled into her desk chair. She had a lot of work to do, but something told her that wasn't enough. To succeed in this new role, she needed to find a way to earn the trust of the other departments she worked with.

Lydia opened up a binder containing a report she had been working on the day before. While it was essential for her to to show competence and authority in the workplace, Lydia also knew that developing relationships beyond the numbers would be essential for long-term success here.

How can I get to know my new colleagues better?

Lydia spent the morning thinking about how to get to know more people across departments. Her game plan included making time for casual conversations both during work hours and afterward—listening carefully to each employee's ideas, offering encouragement when possible, and celebrating any accomplishments.

While questioning an employee about the recent arson certainly wouldn't help foster trust, there was one thing that had to be done.

Lydia carefully pulled out the charred business card she had found in the ashes at the arson site. Mitchell Irving. Marketing department. She opened her desk drawer and thumbed through the staff directory until she found his name. There it was—Mitchell Irving, Marketing Manager. Office 314. Grabbing the damaged card, Lydia made her way quickly through the winding corridors until she reached Mitchell's office. She took a deep breath before knocking firmly on the door.

"Come in!" called a voice from within.

Lydia entered to find a lanky man who looked to be in his late thirties sitting behind a cluttered desk. A snake plant was in the corner of the room, and one of the overhead lights was flickering.

"Mitchell Irving?" she asked.

He looked up, his eyes narrowing slightly. "That's me. And you are?"

"Lydia Boaz, your new CFO. It's nice to meet you." Lydia smiled.

"Oh, hey," said Mitchell, standing up. "Nice to meet you too." He extended a hand, and Lydia reached out and shook it. "How are you finding everything?"

"Oh, great," said Lydia. "Great building; great company; great people to work with."

Mitchell nodded and smiled.

"But hey, I just wanted to stop by because I found your business card at the east side Nod Warehouse which was set on fire." She held out the singed card.

Mitchell's eyes went wide. "What? That's impossible. I've never been to the Nod Warehouse. And…I don't think any of the laborers there would have reason to have my card."

"Yeah, well, I guess it's not impossible," said Lydia, studying him closely. He seemed genuinely shocked and confused. "We all work for the same company, after all."

"That's true," said Mitchell, chuckling sheepishly. He peered at the card for a long while. "It's definitely my card but—I don't know how it would've gotten there. You obviously know I do marketing. I'm rarely out in the field, and I'm almost never at any of our warehouses."

"Yeah, don't worry about it," said Lydia. "Well, it was very nice to meet you. Have a good one!"

Unsure whether to believe him, Lydia slipped the card back into her pocket. She needed more time to think this through. She turned and left Mitchell's office, her mind swirling with unanswered questions.

Lydia returned to her office, lost in thought. Sitting down, she noticed an envelope sitting squarely in the middle of her desk. Her name was written across the front of it.

She picked it up carefully and examined it. I had no return address. Turning it over, she quickly opened the seal and removed a single sheet of paper. It held only a single sentence: Do not get involved in matters that don't concern you.

Lydia's blood seemed to turn to ice in her veins. She looked around but saw no one nearby who could have delivered the letter. Flagging down the office administrator, Alice, she asked, "Did you see who left this on my desk?"

Alice peered at the cryptic note and frowned. "A courier dropped it off about twenty minutes ago."

"A courier?" Lydia's brow furrowed. "Did they say who it was from?"

"No name," Alice replied with a shrug. "Just said it was an anonymous delivery for you. I figured it was harmless, so I left it on your desk."

Lydia nodded, lips pressed in a tight line. This was no coincidence. Someone didn't want her looking into those fires.

Folding the letter, she slipped it into her pocket with Mitchell's business card. A thousand more questions ricocheted through her mind now. She had stumbled onto something bigger than she realized. But was it worth the risk to keep digging?

Lydia sank into her office chair, heart pounding. The anonymous warning echoed in her mind: *Do not get involved in matters that don't concern you.*

She glanced at the half-burned business card bearing Mitchell Irving's name, evidence she had taken from the Nod Warehouse arson site. When she confronted Mitchell about it, he claimed to have no knowledge of ever visiting that facility. Was he lying? Or was someone trying to frame him? Or was it merely a happenstance—one of the laborers at the warehouse had Mitchell's business card for one reason or the other?

She thought back to her conversation with Delilah last night. Her daughter's encouragement to remain brave and to seek the truth. Lydia wished Michelle were here now to offer guidance. Running her hands through her hair, Lydia let out a shaky breath. The right thing to do was clear. She had to keep searching for answers, no matter the risk.

Lydia carefully folded the letter and tucked it into her pocket next to the business card.

Standing, she gathered her things to head home, resolute but wary. She would need to watch her back now. But how could she ignore the silent plea of the ashes, still begging for justice? The truth was out there somewhere.

CHAPTER FOUR

The warm, golden glow of the setting sun filled Delilah's apartment as she and Michelle clinked their wine glasses in a toast.

Michelle was fighting hard to hold back a smile.

"Michelle, what's going on?" Delilah asked. "You've got that mischievous smirk you always wear when you're up to something."

"You know me too well," said Michelle, slowly and cryptically, swirling the wine in her glass. "You're right. There's something I've been wanting to tell you."

"Well, what is it?" Delilah asked, dying to know what was going on.

Michelle held up her left hand, displaying a sparkling diamond banded around her ring finger.

"Oh my god!" Delilah screamed.

"I'm getting married!" Michelle screamed back.

They jumped around in the kitchen and hugged.

Delilah grabbed Michelle's hand to get a closer look at the ring. "It's beautiful! I'm surprised I didn't notice that big rock on your finger!"

"I was hiding it from you," said Michelle. "Couldn't have you figuring it out before I told you."

The two women laughed.

Delilah demanded that Michelle tell her everything she had planned for her upcoming wedding, and Michelle happily obliged, telling Delilah she'd be a big part of those plans since she was the maid of honor. Delilah happily accepted.

As the excitement from the engagement news died down, the two sat on the couch as the gentle hum of the city outside created a soothing backdrop to their intimate conversation.

The two reminisced about old times and shared stories of their latest adventures.

"Michelle, I'm so glad we could catch up," Delilah said, her eyes glistening with emotion.

"Me too, Delilah," Michelle replied, squeezing her friend's hand. "I know we live thousands of miles apart now, but remember, I'm always here when you need me."

"Thank you," said Delilah, feeling a wave of gratitude wash over her. "You have no idea how much that means to me."

It wasn't long before their conversation turned toward Lydia and the mysterious arsonist, and Delilah felt a pang of worry for her mother's safety.

"Michelle," she asked hesitantly, "do you think my mom will be okay? I mean, with everything that's going on with the fires...I just don't want anything to happen to her."

"Your mom will be careful, Delilah," Michelle assured her, her voice filled with conviction. "I have no doubt that she'll rise to whatever challenges come her way. And besides, she has you. And you won't let anything happen to her."

Delilah smiled. She couldn't argue with that.

THE STEAMING AROMA of freshly brewed coffee filled the air as Lydia Boaz entered the cozy coffee shop in the heart of New York City. The soft chatter of other patrons and the clinking of cups on saucers created a comforting ambiance. She was excited at the prospect of seeing her daughter's close friend, Michelle Harper.

"Lydia!" Michelle called, her voice cutting through the din as she approached with open arms. They embraced warmly, their smiles genuine and welcoming.

"Michelle, it's so good to see you," Lydia said as they separated and found a quiet corner table. "You're like a ray of sunshine on this hectic day."

"Thanks, Lydia. I'm just glad I could be here for Delilah," Michelle responded, her eyes sparkling warmly. "So, tell me about your new job as CFO, and what brings you to this arson investigation?"

Lydia hesitated for a moment, her mind racing with doubts and concerns. "Well, it's been quite a whirlwind. I want to make a real difference in the company, but the timing of these fires couldn't have been worse. I'm unsure how to navigate this situation while balancing my role as CFO. Not to mention, it's scary that we have an arsonist on the prowl."

Michelle leaned in, her expression attentive. "First of all, trust yourself, Lydia. You're an incredibly capable woman. And remember, you don't have to tackle everything alone. Lean on those around you, especially those who care for you deeply."

"Thank you, Michelle," Lydia replied, her voice filled with gratitude. "I'll do my best to keep that in mind."

As the conversation continued, Lydia felt her concerns lessen. Michelle's words of encouragement and support resonated deeply.

"Lydia, I've known you for years, and I know how dedicated you are to your work. But there's more to being a great CFO than just being good at numbers. As your daughter Delilah once told me, 'Stay positive. Connect and communicate. Value your work.'"

"Delilah said that?" Lydia asked, surprised by her daughter's insight.

"Indeed." Michelle smiled warmly. "And she's right. By staying positive, you invite good things to come your way. Remember, you're in this position because you have what it takes. And you have others around you who will help."

"Thanks so much for your advice," said Lydia, feeling encouraged. Then she noticed a shiny diamond ring on

Michelle's left hand. She motioned down at the ring with her eyes. "Is that what I think it is?"

Michelle grinned and nodded. "I just told Delilah last night!"

"Congratulations!" Lydia gushed. "I absolutely love that ring!"

"Thanks Lydia!"

THE FOLLOWING DAY, Lydia couldn't shake Michelle's advice from her mind. Though Rico had told her that she didn't need to participate in the arson investigation, Lydia now felt compelled to do so. It was an opportunity to connect with her boss and strengthen her relationships with her colleagues.

She decided it might be a good idea to visit the two facilities that hadn't been attacked, so she got in her car and headed out.

Lydia approached the first facility, Banon Warehouse. She exited her car and circled the imposing structure, and Lydia's keen eyes scanned every inch for any possible leads. She went inside and spoke with security and two different floor managers, asking if they'd seen anything suspicious lately. They all answered no, and Lydia examined the outside of the building one last time before she left. Her pulse quickened as she neared the rear of the warehouse and spotted something familiar—shoe prints in the mud, their tread of little circles unmistakable. A surge of adrenaline shot through her.

"Could it really be this simple?" she whispered, excitement bubbling within her. She then hurried off to the next nearest facility, Carmel Warehouse.

Upon arrival, Lydia wasted no time scouring the premises, fueled by her earlier discovery. But despite her best efforts, there were no shoe prints with circles to be found. Again, she asked around inside about suspicious activity, but no one had seen anything of note.

With a heavy sigh, Lydia returned to her office, her mind whirling with questions and possibilities. Sitting down at her desk, she allowed herself a moment to reflect on the day's events and the lessons learned. Trusting herself had led her to find vital clues in the investigation, but it also opened up a myriad of uncertainties.

"Who is behind these arsons? What is their ultimate goal?" she pondered, frustration gnawing at her.

But even as doubt threatened to consume her, Lydia knew that she must press on, for the sake of the company and her colleagues. As she prepared herself for the challenges ahead, she felt a sense of pride in her accomplishments that day—after all, she had made up her mind to commit to the arson investigation, and that was certainly more than expected.

And as Lydia Boaz prepared to face the unknown, she had no doubt in her mind that she would rise to meet the challenges.

When Lydia arrived at work the following day, the news she heard made her freeze. The Banon Warehouse had been burned to the ground overnight.

"Another fire?" Lydia whispered. She remembered the shoe prints with the circles she had discovered at Banon Warehouse. *But not at Carmel.*

While the shoe prints had been curious but not necessarily incriminating before, this changed everything. It was entirely plausible that a field employee or even a police officer or detective would've visited all the arson sites. But the fact that this person was at the site before it burned down was telling. Not only that, but the prints weren't at the other site that hadn't been attacked.

"Whoever wears those shoes…they're likely the arsonist," Lydia realized, her breath catching in her throat. She decided to keep this information to herself for now, uncertain how to proceed.

As Lydia sat at her desk, her thoughts zoomed back to Mitchell Irving, the man whose business card had been found at the scene of a fire. Could he be the one wearing those shoes? The idea nagged at her, refusing to leave her mind.

"I need to see him again," she murmured, her fingers drumming nervously on her desk. Standing up abruptly, she strode out of her office.

Lydia took a deep breath and knocked on Mitchell Irving's office door. This was no time to second-guess herself; she needed answers, and she needed them now.

"Come in!" Mitchell called, his voice smooth but detached. Lydia pushed the door open and stepped inside. "What can I do for you, Lydia?"

"Hi, Mitchell. I have a few questions about the marketing budget," she said, leaning against the edge of his desk. She glanced around the room, taking in every detail—the neatly organized papers, the polished surface of the desk, the faint scent of cologne lingering in the air. Her senses were heightened, her mind reeling with possibilities.

"Of course," Mitchell replied. He opened one of his desk drawers and pulled out a folder stuffed with papers. He opened the folders and sifted through the documents until finally finding the financial report in question. "Are we spending more, less, or the same amount of money for marketing this year?"

"Actually, that's what I wanted to ask you," Lydia responded, her voice steady despite the adrenaline. Mitchell looked at her momentarily, then turned his attention back to the report.

"Well, it seems our marketing budget has increased by about ten percent since last year," he said after a brief pause. "We've been investing more in digital advertising and targeted campaigns, which has increased costs."

"Interesting," Lydia mused, her eyes darting down to Mitchell's feet. She wondered if the tread on the bottom of his shoes was none other than a scattering of little circles. But there was no way to see the bottom of his shoe, no way to confirm if the tread matched the prints she had found. The frustration bubbled within her, but she kept her composure.

"Thanks for the information, Mitchell," she said, forcing a smile and standing up straight. "I'll be sure to keep that in mind as we move forward."

"Anytime, Lydia," Mitchell replied, wearing a faint smile. As she turned to leave, she felt a nagging suspicion that he knew more than he was letting on.

Back in her own office, Lydia's mind wouldn't stop reeling. She needed to find a way to see the bottom of Mitchell's shoes, but how? And what if he wasn't the arsonist? She had so many questions it was driving her nuts.

As she thought about how in the world she could see the bottom of Mitchell's shoes, an idea started to form, and Lydia smiled as it crystallized in her mind. With a household item that could be found at any drugstore, there might just be a way to get his footprints.

When she left for the day, she went to a local drugstore and bought the item, and she made sure she took it with her to work the next day.

The following morning was spent scheming the best way to carry out her mission. Her fingers drummed impatiently on her desk as she mulled over her plan. The idea was risky, but it just might work. As soon as she finished her morning tasks, she checked to see what time Mitchell usually went to lunch. *Eleven-thirty.* With her purse in tow, she loitered near Mitchell's office, pretending to check on the other departments nearby.

When Lydia saw Mitchell leave for lunch, she made her move. With a quick glance around to ensure no one was watching, she dashed over to his desk, reached into her purse and pulled out a bottle of baby powder. She twisted the cap open. She sprinkled a thin layer of the fine white dust in front of his chair, the particles dancing through the air, casting a soft glow before settling on the light gray linoleum floor. The barely noticeable contrast created a subtle trap for Mitchell's shoes, one that Lydia hoped would supply the answers she needed.

Let's see what you're hiding now.

LYDIA NERVOUSLY WATCHED as Mitchell returned from his lunch break. As he approached his desk and sat down, the moment of truth had arrived: would the baby powder reveal the secrets hidden beneath his shoes?

Mitchell shifted in his chair, unknowingly pressing his shoe soles into the fine white dust. She watched without breathing or blinking, her pulse pounding, knowing it was only a matter of time before she had her answer.

Lydia waited until Mitchell had left for the day, and then she crept into his office to examine his shoe prints in the baby powder.

Lydia saw that the shoe prints had a common design on the bottom—a series of plus signs arranged in an orderly pattern, almost like a complex jigsaw puzzle. She immediately knew it didn't match the tread she'd seen at the arson sites.

A sigh of relief escaped her lips as she exhaled, considering Mitchell might not be their man after all. She quickly disposed of the evidence, blowing at the powder and rubbing her foot over it to smear it away.

"Missed you more," she muttered, unwilling to let go just yet. After a moment, they reluctantly separated, grinning broadly.

Delilah was bursting with emotion at the sight of Jobe. She was relieved to have him back with her, and she found herself overwhelmed by the memories they had shared before her departure. Even though many years had passed since they first met, she was reminded of all the joys, sorrows, and adventures they had experienced throughout their friendship.

Delilah felt warm tears prickling at the corner of her eyes as she looked into Jobe's kind face; it seemed like no time had passed at all since she'd left. No matter how much time and distance separated them, nothing could break the bond between them—and Delilah was grateful for that.

"Come on, let's get you out of here," Delilah said, grabbing his hand and leading him toward the exit.

As they walked side by side, Delilah noticed how happy and comfortable she felt around Jobe. It was as if nothing had changed between them, even though months had passed since they last saw each other. While they had grown up together and shared a few romantic moments over the years, the core of their relationship had always been a close friendship. While Delilah often wondered if more was ever meant for them, just having Jobe as a friend often seemed like enough.

"Jobe, you won't believe the news—Michelle's getting married!" Delilah gushed as they settled into her car.

"Really? That's amazing! Wow, we have so much to catch up on."

"Absolutely!" Delilah agreed, so excited she could burst. As she drove, they chatted about everything that had happened during their time apart—the good things, the bad things, and everything in between. The conversation flowed effortlessly, a testament to the enduring strength of their friendship.

"By the way," Jobe said, suddenly serious, "I've been thinking a lot about your mom's situation at work that you told me about in your letter. I might have an idea that could help."

"Really?" Delilah asked, her curiosity piqued. She knew how perceptive he could be, especially when it came to complex problems.

"Let's discuss it with her over coffee tomorrow morning," he suggested, his eyes twinkling with excitement. "I know a thing or two about arsonists, naturally."

Of course, Delilah thought, surprised that she hadn't thought of it before. *Before that flood changed his path, Jobe used to be a firefighter.*

Delilah felt a surge of hope as she pulled into her apartment's parking lot. With Jobe by her side, anything was possible, and he might have some helpful advice for her mother in dealing with the fires.

"Well, it's not O'Malley's," said Delilah once Jobe had settled in, "but there's an Irish Pub around the corner if you're interested."

Jobe nodded eagerly. "Sounds great!"

They made their way to the pub, a modest establishment with a sign out front featuring an orange and white harp emblem. Inside, they were greeted by Gaelic music and the warm scent of whiskey in the air. The walls were decorated in vibrant yellow and green wallpaper with old Irish family crests framed on them. Bartenders behind the bar smiled at them as they settled into two stools near the window overlooking the street.

Delilah ordered a pint of Guinness while Jobe asked for whiskey on ice. They clinked glasses in celebration over their reunion before taking a long sip from their drinks and sighing contentedly in relief.

"So tell me more about your new position," said Jobe, swirling his whiskey until the ice rattled and and clinked.

"I'm the Communications Lead," Delilah said proudly. "So I work with the marketing and sales departments. Right now, I'm overseeing a marketing campaign. It's challenging but really fun."

"A marketing campaign, huh? Sounds exciting."

"Oh, it is," said Delilah. "Trust me. How about you? Is teaching everything you thought it would be?"

"Definitely," said Jobe with a chuckle. "And more."

The conversation flowed freely between them as they continued to discuss work, school, family drama, and whatever else came to mind—all while laughing non-stop for hours at a time as if nothing had changed since the last time they saw each other.

Delilah couldn't help but feel like she was back in her college days—running around town with Jobe. They had a connection that defied description; it was like they could finish each other's thoughts, feeling each other's feelings so deeply that there didn't seem to be any room for anything else.

They talked about their dreams, hopes, and ambitions for the future, and how they could strive to make them happen.

"I really want to work my way up to a place where I can do some good in the world," Delilah confided in Jobe. "I've moved around a lot: from back home, to Europe, and then to New York, and I've always been independent—always loved to travel. So I think the end goal is to have the financial freedom to work anywhere in the world, while at the same time making a big enough impact to really be able to help people."

"Delilah that's amazing," said Jobe, his face saying he was genuinely in awe. His mouth hung open and his eyes squinted as if pondering the importance of Delilah's words.

Delilah felt such an immense sense of comfort being around Jobe—she trusted him wholeheartedly. She truly believed that Jobe saw her as a friend first and foremost, which was why she appreciated him so much; having him as a friend felt best, she convinced herself. But that didn't explain the butterflies she'd felt the last time they had kissed. Every time they kissed.

As they finished their drinks, Delilah wondered how their story would end. She felt as if things had come full circle with Jobe and that all of her questions about them were finally answered. But there were some things left unsaid that neither of them seemed ready to tackle.

Delilah wasn't sure what the future held for her and Jobe, but she was willing to find out. For now, it was enough to just enjoy being in his company without worrying about the consequences or making any plans for their relationship.

As they left the pub hand-in-hand, Delilah knew one thing for sure: even if their story didn't end up with a happily ever after, she would always be thankful for having such an amazing friend by her side through it all.

THE SMELL OF freshly brewed coffee filled the air as Lydia ordered a hot drink at her favorite local coffee shop. She sat down at a table, glancing around as she adjusted the purple shawl draped over her blouse. She noted the familiar faces of the regulars and the warm, inviting atmosphere. Delilah arrived shortly after, with Jobe in tow, both of them wearing broad smiles.

"Hey, Jobe!" Lydia gasped when he walked. "It's so good to see you!"

"Lydia! It's been too long," said Jobe, wrapping her in a hug.

Lydia held both of Jobe's hands, smiling at him and looking him in the eyes. "You know what? I've always told Delilah that you and she are—"

"Mom!" Delilah interrupted. "Stop! You can't do that!"

"Okay, okay," said Lydia.

They all laughed, and Delilah pulled Jobe toward the front counter with a look of embarrassment on her face. They each ordered a coffee, returned to Lydia's table, and sat down.

"All right, let's get down to business," Lydia began, her tone shifting to a more serious one. "My investigation into the warehouse fires has hit a dead end. We need new leads, and Delilah said you might have an idea."

Jobe nodded thoughtfully before speaking. "Arsonists often return to the scene of the crime. They take pleasure in their work, watching things burn." He paused for a moment, sipping his coffee. "If you stake out the remaining warehouses and can identify who's watching the fire, you might find your arsonist."

"Interesting," Lydia mused, her mind racing through the possibilities. "But how do we know when the next fire will happen?"

"Unfortunately, we don't," Jobe admitted. "But if we're proactive, we might be able to catch the building while it's burning. Assuming the arsonist sticks around to view their handiwork, you might catch them there at the scene."

"Then that's what we'll do." Determination shone in Lydia's eyes, and she could see that same fire reflected in Delilah and Jobe's expressions.

The following day, Lydia took a trip to Carmel Warehouse. Once there, she made her way to the security office.

"I want you to alert me immediately if there's any sign of fire," she instructed, her voice firm. "I'd like to be there in person if and when that happens."

"Understood, Ms. Boaz," the security officer replied.

"Thank you."

Lydia went back to her building, her stomach clenching at the thought of yet another fire. This was risky, but it could lead them to the arsonist.

At that moment, Lydia realized how much she needed people like Jobe and Delilah in her life—individuals who would stand by her side and fight for what was right. Michelle's words of advice echoed in her mind: *Lean on those around you.*

The road ahead was going to be difficult, but with their combined strength, she knew they could prevail.

As she stared out of her office window, she saw a truck on the streets below with a Phoenix painted on it, the wings of the mythical creature outstretched as it soared. And she wondered, in a moment of rumination, if she tackled this arson investigation, if she too would soar to new heights.

IT WAS AN important day for Delilah. She was determined to excel at her new job, and she knew just what she needed to make that happen. Her mother, Lydia, had taught her the benefits of staying positive, and Delilah herself had recently come to realize how important it was to connect and communicate with her coworkers—and that's what this day was for.

SHE HAD SET up team-building exercises with the departments she worked closely with, and she was excited to see how everyone got along. As the Communications Lead, she worked with both the marketing and sales departments, and it was also her job to manage the public perception of the company or, in other words, its brand. She could only be successful at doing this if everyone was working together.

"All right, team! Gather 'round!" Delilah called to her colleagues, clapping her hands with enthusiasm. Her eyes sparkled with excitement as she motioned for them to join her in the conference room.

"Today, we're going to strengthen our bond as a team through some fun activities I've planned," Delilah announced.

"Like what?" one of her colleagues asked, curiosity piqued.

Delilah grinned. "First up, we're going to do a group problem-solving activity, followed by an improv skit where each of us has to act out different roles." Delilah smirked mischievously. "And then one final activity to make sure we all trust each other."

"Sounds interesting," another colleague chimed in.

"Great! Let's get started." Delilah clapped her hands once more, but the room was filled with groans and languid smiles.

"All right, everyone, let's get started," Delilah announced.

In the group problem-solving activity, Delilah watched as her teammates cooperated to untangle themselves from a human knot, brainstorming ideas and strategies to free themselves without breaking physical contact.

"Keep it up, guys! You're almost there!" Delilah cheered as she saw the progress they were making.

Then, it was time for the improv skits. Delilah assigned different roles to each participant, urging them to step out of their comfort zones and embrace the challenge. As they acted out their scenes, the room filled with laughter and applause at their creative performances.

"Wow, that was amazing!" Delilah exclaimed as one skit came to an end. "You guys are all so talented!"

Finally, it was time for the trust fall. As Delilah organized her team into pairs, she couldn't help but feel a sense of pride in her ability to bring people together. With every successful fall and catch, laughter and cheers echoed throughout the room. Colleagues who had barely spoken to each other before were now actively communicating and relying on one another.

"Nice catch, Mark!" Delilah shouted as one teammate confidently caught his partner.

"Thanks, Delilah," he replied, grinning. "This is actually pretty fun."

As the team-building event drew to a close, Delilah felt a wave of satisfaction wash over her. She had successfully united her colleagues, fostering connections through teamwork and empathy. Her leadership skills had shone through, and she knew she had made a positive impact on her team.

"Thank you, Delilah," said Tyler as he filed out of the conference room, a broad smile on his face. "This was a fantastic experience. We should do this more often."

"Of course! I'm glad you enjoyed it," Delilah replied, her own smile lighting up the room.

"Delilah, this was amazing!" exclaimed Priya. "I've never felt so connected to everyone before. Thank you for organizing this."

"Seriously, Delilah," Jenia chimed in. "That was the most fun I've had here in years."

As Delilah listened to their words, she felt proud of the difference she was making. She knew good connections were the cornerstone of any successful team, and it warmed her heart to create this bond with her colleagues.

AT WORK, LYDIA sat at her desk, pouring over the company's financial reports. Her brow furrowed as she scrutinized each figure, searching for inconsistencies or anomalies. The case continued to tug at her thoughts, a constant reminder of the danger lurking in the shadows.

"Lydia! W-We've just been contacted by the security department at Carmel Warehouse!" Alice rushed into the room, her face pale with fear. "The building is on fire!"

Lydia's heart dropped to the pit of her stomach as the words registered in her mind. Every moment counted now. With a swift nod, she grabbed her keys and bolted from the office, leaving behind the safety of her workspace for the fiery chaos that awaited her.

"Stay safe, Lydia!" Alice called after her.

Lydia ran through the halls and out to her car, her mind racing as fast as her footsteps.

The tires screeched as Lydia sped away from the office and toward the Carmel processing center. Her hands gripped the steering wheel so tightly that her knuckles turned white while her thoughts churned in a whirlwind of fear and determination.

Please let everyone be okay.

As she neared the facility, black smoke billowed into the sky, painting an ominous picture against the otherwise clear day. Lydia's car skidded to a halt in the gravel parking lot, sending a cloud of dust into the air. The burning Carmel center loomed before her like a towering inferno, its flames licking at the sky with an insatiable hunger. She could feel the intense heat on her face, and as she stared at the rapidly disintegrating structure, her heart sank with despair.

"Please tell me everyone got out!" she shouted over the roar of the fire to the nearest security officer, who was trying to keep the onlookers at a safe distance.

"Yes, ma'am, we've evacuated all employees. The police and fire department have been called. They're on their way," he replied, his face grim under the circumstances.

"Thank God," she muttered, relief settling her nerves before the gravity of the situation returned. Her sharp analytical mind began searching for answers. As Lydia scanned the crowd, her eyes were drawn to an unusual figure standing not far away from the burning building. It was Mitchell Irving, his gaze locked on the dancing flames.

CHAPTER SIX

The unpleasant smell of charred wood lingered in Lydia's nostrils as she strode through her office building. She could still see Mitchell Irving standing just outside the perimeter of the latest fire scene, the roaring flames reflected in his eyes.

Lydia shook her head, her dark hair dancing over her shoulders. The image gnawed at her relentlessly, refusing to be forgotten. Maybe it was just like Jobe had said: arsonists liked to admire their handiwork.

It's time to pay him another visit.

The door to Mitchell's office was slightly ajar, and without so much as a knock, Lydia pushed it open. Mitchell looked up from his desk, surprise flickering across his face as he recognized her.

"Lydia! What can I do for you?"

"Can you tell me why exactly you were present at the site of the fire yesterday?" Lydia wasted no time getting to the point, her eyes narrowing suspiciously.

"Ah, yes. I was scheduled to visit that location for a district meeting with our marketing department. We were discussing company goals," Mitchell explained, his brows knitting together. "When I arrived, the place was already ablaze. Is something wrong?"

Lydia studied his face, searching for any signs of deceit. Is your story going to check out?

"Just curious," said Lydia.

Mitchell nodded. "Got it. Well, look, you've asked me about the fires a couple of times now. You don't think…" Mitchell trailed off, his eyes squinting. "You don't think I might've had something to do with it, right?"

"No, Mitchell," Lydia lied. "Just let me know if you hear anything."

"Of course."

Lydia knew she couldn't rule out Mitchell just yet. After a tense moment, she nodded curtly and left his office.

Mitchell said he had a meeting at that facility, and this information was easily verifiable, so she sought out his manager. She found him in the break room, pouring himself a cup of coffee.

"Hey, I'm Lydia," she said, smiling and extending a hand. "CFO. I think we've seen each other around."

The man smiled and shook her hand. "Oh, yeah, that's right. How are you?"

"I'm well, thanks. I just wanted to ask you, since I know you're Mitchell's manager—Mitchell Irving. I need to know if Mitchell was scheduled for a meeting at the facility that caught fire yesterday."

The manager looked startled by her question but nodded. "Yes, he was supposed to be there for a meeting. Why?" He scratched his head.

"Thank you," Lydia replied. "Oh, it's nothing, really. I'm just trying to keep track of all the meetings we have around here."

"Yeah, there's always some sort of meeting happening," the man said.

"Exactly," said Lydia. "It's crazy! Well, thanks again. Have a good one!"

Mitchell's name was cleared, at least for now. But the feeling in her gut persisted. She needed to meet with Lucky B to see if he had any leads. This arsonist needed to be caught before any more damage could be done.

As Lydia walked through the busy office, her thoughts raced. The evidence she had collected so far seemed to lead nowhere. And yet, something about Mitchell nagged at her. What was it that she couldn't see?

She shook her head in frustration, pushing aside her doubts for the moment. Right now, she needed to focus on finding Lucky B and uncovering any information he might have. Lydia knew she couldn't afford to waste any more time. As she headed toward the exit, she readied herself for the challenges that lay ahead, determined to bring the arsonist to justice.

She hopped in her car and drove to Lucky B's headquarters adjacent to the fire station.

Lydia's heels clicked against the linoleum floor of the building where Lucky B's office was situated. She walked through the open door to find him and another man hunched over a table, brows furrowed as they examined a large map.

"Find anything new?" Lydia asked.

Lucky B looked up, his expression serious. "Ah, Lydia. It's good to see you. This is Detective Sturm, who's working this case with me."

The man extended a hand, his hardened face producing a stern mien, even if he was smiling. "Nice to meet you, Lydia."

Lydia shook his hand. "Nice to meet you too, detective."

"Well, I have to get going," Detective Sturm said. "I'm sure we'll all talk soon." He dipped his head and headed out the door.

"So, what do we know?" asked Lydia.

"The pattern is clear," said Lucky B, gesturing to the map, the locations of the fires marked with a red pen. "Only buildings associated with New York Meat are being attacked. This makes it more likely to be an employee."

"Interesting," Lydia mused, leaning closer. "Someone not happy with their job, perhaps?"

"It's very possible," Lucky B replied, and he blew out a sigh. "Of course, a former employee makes even more sense..." The investigator trailed off.

As they discussed the implications of the lack of a clear pattern, Lydia found herself growing more and more determined to solve the case. She fired off question after question, eager to learn the ins and outs of investigative techniques from Lucky B. Her pen flew across her notepad, jotting down notes on evidence collection, motive analysis, and suspect profiling.

"Thanks for showing me all this," Lydia said, sincere gratitude in her voice. "I want to make sure I'm doing everything possible to help."

"Hey, that's what I'm here for," Lucky B replied, a small smile tugging at the corners of his mouth. "We'll get them, Lydia. It's only a matter of time."

DELILAH REVIEWED HER notes, her hands steady despite the nerves fluttering in her stomach. This presentation had to go well—she'd worked too hard to let it fall flat. She stepped back a bit and faced her colleagues gathered around the boardroom table.

"Good morning, everyone. Today, I'd like to share some innovative ideas I've been developing to streamline our communications," Delilah began, her voice clear and confident. She handed out documentation, showcasing a new company messaging software that would be adopted in the coming weeks.

Her coworkers leaned in, their eyes locked on their handouts as she explained her plans to roll out the new company email system. As Delilah spoke, she felt a surge of energy electrify her. This was it—her moment to shine and prove her worth to the company.

A smile played on Delilah's lips as she watched her colleagues exchange impressed glances. She knew she'd hit the mark, and she allowed herself to savor this moment of satisfaction.

As the meeting continued, Delilah's mind drifted to her mother, Lydia, who was grappling with a complex investigation. The thought filled her with a sense of resolve, knowing that they were both fighting to make a difference in their own ways.

Delilah went over the new software explained on the documents she'd handed out, emphasizing key points and captivating her audience with her eloquence and insight. Every word, every movement was carefully chosen for maximum impact, and she could feel the admiration of her coworkers growing with each passing moment.

"By implementing this new system, our internal communication will be faster and more reliable," Delilah said, her voice steady and commanding. She looked around the room, pleased to see nodding heads and thoughtful expressions on the faces of those present. It was clear they recognized the value of her ideas, and she couldn't help but feel proud.

LYDIA SAT IN her office, her fingers drumming on the desk as she pondered the information she'd gleaned from Lucky B. The clues she'd gathered at the burn sites swirled in her mind: the strange footprints, the faint smell of gasoline lingering in the air, and the unsettling sight of Mitchell staring into the flames.

Determined to get to the bottom of the arson mystery, Lydia made a decision.

She stood up, straightened her blazer, and marched determinedly to Rico's office. She was ready to take on the challenge— and prove once and for all that she was worthy of this assignment.

As Lydia made her way down the hallway, she tried not to think about the daunting task ahead of her. She arrived outside Rico's office door, calmed herself, then opened it slowly and stepped inside. The room felt larger than life—polished wood floors stretching out into an impressive workspace complete with shelves lined with awards from prestigious organizations around the world.

Rico sat behind his desk, his gaze fixed intently on a stack of papers before him.

"Rico, I'd like to spearhead this investigation. I know you said I could hand it off to Diego, but I think I'm up for it."

Rico smiled warmly. "Really? Are you sure?"

Lydia winked. "Positive. I'm sure Diego has more on his plate than I do. And like you said, it'll be good to get a fresh pair of eyes on it."

"That's great, Lydia. I appreciate this very much."

"It's my pleasure, sir," Lydia replied. "Well, I think it's time we hold a company meeting. I want to keep management updated on the arson investigation."

"Understood, Lydia," Rico replied, his tone serious and concerned. "I'll arrange for the meeting to take place tomorrow morning. Your dedication to getting to the bottom of this matter is commendable."

As Lydia left, she felt a renewed sense of purpose. She knew she was close to cracking the case, and she wasn't going to let anything stand in her way. Tomorrow's meeting would be the first step toward bringing the arsonist to justice.

But as Lydia reflected on her progress, she couldn't shake the nagging feeling that there was something she was missing. What could it be? And why did Mitchell Irving's presence at the latest fire continue to haunt her thoughts, even though his alibi had checked out? These questions swirled around in her mind, like embers in the smoldering ruins of the buildings she'd investigated. With each unanswered question, Lydia felt herself being drawn further into the labyrinth of intrigue and danger that surrounded the arson cases. But she knew she couldn't turn back—she was in too deep now, and the stakes were higher than ever.

Lydia entered the conference room the next day greeted by the faces of the company's top executives. She took her place at the head of the table, her heart racing but her demeanor calm and collected.

"Thank you all for coming on such short notice," Lydia began, her voice steady and commanding. "As you're well aware, our company has been targeted by an arsonist. Rico has asked me to discover who's behind this and bring them to justice."

Rico nodded appreciatively. "Lydia, we can't thank you enough for taking this on. With everything else we have to manage, your dedication to solving this case is invaluable."

"Indeed," chimed in Diego, the COO. "Your expertise and commitment have not gone unnoticed."

Lydia acknowledged their gratitude with a nod, then dove into the evidence she'd gathered so far. As she detailed each piece of information, the room waited in quiet reverence, the tension thick. Yet she held back on mentioning the shoe prints, feeling that there was more to uncover before revealing that piece of the puzzle.

"It's worth mentioning that we're down ten percent on expenses from last year—with the exception of the damages from the fires, of course. But it's good to know that without this unexpected arson, we're right where we need to be."

Lydia looked around the table, watching as the other executives exchanged concerned glances.

"Lydia, I don't know what we would do without you," Rico said earnestly, reflecting the sentiment of everyone in the room. "We'll support you in any way we can to ensure these attacks come to an end."

"Thank you," Lydia replied, touched by their faith in her abilities. "I won't let you down."

As the meeting adjourned, Lydia strode from the room with renewed vigor, more determined than ever. The fire within her burned brighter, fueled by the support of her colleagues and her unwavering resolve to put an end to the arsonist's reign of terror.

With each step she took, Lydia knew she was getting closer to the truth. But as she continued her investigation, she couldn't help but wonder what other secrets lay in wait, ready to be uncovered. As her mind raced with unanswered questions and possibilities, Lydia knew that the path ahead would be treacherous, filled with twists and turns at every corner. But no matter how dark or dangerous the journey became, she was ready to face whatever challenges lay ahead and bring the arsonist to justice.

As the flames of intrigue continued to flicker and dance in her mind, Lydia prepared herself for the next stage of her relentless pursuit—a pursuit that would, perhaps, take her deeper into the heart of darkness than she'd ever ventured before.

Lydia's heart pounded in her chest as she walked back to her office, thoughts running wild. The footprints at the arson sites haunted her, as did Mitchell Irving's presence at the most recent fire.

Maybe I shouldn't be worrying about Mitchell. She shook her head to clear her thoughts. *The arsonist is probably someone I don't know.*

"Lydia!" a coworker called out from outside her office, jolting her from her intense focus. "You've been working non-stop! Are you sure you're okay?"

"Absolutely," she replied, her voice steely with determination. "I need to find answers, and I will."

Back at her desk, Lydia took a moment to glance out of the window, hoping for a brief distraction from her thoughts. And that's when she saw it again: the truck with the Phoenix painted on its side. The majestic creature seemed to leap right out of the metal, its wings outstretched, fiery feathers shimmering in the fading evening light. The Phoenix seemed to embody opportunity itself, soaring through the air and leaving the mundane world behind.

The sight stirred something deep within Lydia, a yearning for adventure and discovery that had lurked dormant beneath her practical exterior. It was as if the Phoenix was urging her onward, whispering its secrets on the wind that ruffled its fiery feathers.

"What am I missing?" she muttered, shaking off her reverie and turning her gaze back to the office. She knew every moment counted, and she couldn't afford to get lost in daydreams when there was so much work to be done.

The evening dragged on, and Lydia, deep in thought, barely noticed the soft footsteps approaching her office. The door creaked open and Alice slipped inside with an air of secrecy.

"Lydia," she whispered urgently, "I was handed this earlier today."

Alice extended a crisp white envelope toward Lydia. Lydia took the envelope, wondering what she might find inside.

"Who gave this to you?" Lydia asked, her voice serious and low.

"I don't know," Alice admitted, biting her lip. "They were wearing sunglasses and a hat. I didn't get a good look at their face. Something seemed really off about them."

Lydia frowned, her fingers tracing the edges of the unmarked envelope. With a quick nod of thanks, she waited for Alice to leave before tearing it open and scanning the message scrawled inside.

"Meet me at the latest arson site.
I have something you need to see.

- Lucky B"

CHAPTER SEVEN

Delilah's pen flew across her notebook, jotting down notes to remind herself of the critical areas of focus as Communications Lead: work with the marketing department to ensure marketing copy and public perception of the company aligns with their brand; optimize internal and external communication of the sales department. Her heart raced with excitement for the evening ahead—dinner with Jobe. Yet, as she glanced at the clock, she couldn't help but feel melancholy, knowing it was his last night in New York.

Time to wind down and have some fun. She closed her notebook and grabbed her jacket.

As she drove home, her thoughts danced between excitement and sorrow. She recalled Jobe's laughter, his patient nature, and the way he always managed to calm her down when stress threatened to overwhelm her. His visit had been a week, but it had gone by way too fast.

When she got back to her place, she took a shower, got dressed for a night out, and she and Jobe set out.

A gust of wind swept through the city streets as they ventured out into the night. Delilah noticed how well Jobe fit into this bustling metropolis—despite being in a strange new place, he seemed so at ease with himself and his surroundings. They weaved through the crowd of pedestrians and shopkeepers on their way to dinner, their laughter mingling with the sound of honking horns and street performers' music filling the air around them.

The glowing lights from neon signs illuminated their path as they passed by restaurants and small eateries that promised exotic flavors. Delilah pointed out different stores from her favorite clothing brands to ice cream shops that she loved, excited to show these places to Jobe.

The cozy restaurant they had chosen bustled with life, its warm glow casting a golden hue over the intimate tables.

As they sat down, their conversation flowed easily, filled with laughter and vulnerability as they recalled their old memories.

"Remember when we were walking through the woods, and I stepped on that wasp nest?" Delilah asked, her eyes widening at the memory.

Jobe started laughing. "We took off running, and they chased us!"

"Yeah, but you protected me," Delilah reminded him. "When we couldn't run anymore, you shielded me with your body so they couldn't sting me—and they stung you all up!"

Jobe shrugged like it wasn't a big deal. "I only got stung a few times."

As their conversation became more intimate, they leaned closer, their voices barely audible above the din of the restaurant. Their eyes locked in a moment of connection that made the hairs on Delilah's neck begin to stand. Their hands reached across the table, their fingers intertwining when they met.

"Delilah," Jobe whispered, his eyes never leaving hers. "No matter where life takes us, I hope we'll always make time for each other. I'll always make time for you."

The intensity of the moment left her breathless, and she realized just how much she would miss him. Delilah wished she had the power to stop time.

"Thank you, Jobe," she murmured, squeezing his hand. "Life's always better with you in it."

Jobe winked and then showed her a little smirk. "Well, what's next?"

Delilah knew that look well. He was thinking about a night out on the town, just like she was. She smiled at him. "Let's see where the night takes us."

The night air was electric as Delilah and Jobe walked side by side, bar-hopping along the crowded streets of New York. The city pulsed with life, its energy infectious. Pausing at the entrance of a dimly lit jazz club, they exchanged excited glances before pushing their way inside.

"Here's to new adventures," Jobe declared as they clinked glasses, sipping on their drinks while swaying to the hypnotic rhythm of the live music. Hours passed in a blur of laughter and conversation, each drink making them feel more alive than the last.

As the clock struck midnight, they stumbled back to Delilah's apartment, their steps slightly unsteady but their spirits high. Once inside, they collapsed onto the couch, their bodies close and warm, as a comfortable silence settled between them.

Delilah felt like taking a leap of faith, to embrace the intimacy that had been building between them all evening. Rising from the couch, nerves fluttering in her stomach, she excused herself to the bathroom. But when she came out she found Jobe fast asleep on the sofa, his breaths slow and even. A bittersweet smile tugged at her lips, and she draped a blanket over him and retreated to her bedroom, her dreams filled with whispered promises and lingering touches.

Morning light filtered through the curtains as Delilah awoke, her thoughts entwined with memories of the night before. Padding into the kitchen, she found Jobe already awake, a sheepish grin on his face as he prepared breakfast.

"Hey, I'm sorry about last night," he said, rubbing the back of his neck. "I guess I had one too many."

"Jobe, it's fine," Delilah reassured him with a smile. "I'm just glad we had such a great night."

As they shared their meal, Delilah reflected on the almost moments and unspoken desires that had colored their evening. Despite the uncertainty of what lay ahead, she felt a deep sense of gratitude for the connection they had forged.

"Delilah," Jobe said softly, breaking her from her thoughts. "I have to catch a taxi to the airport soon."

"I know." Delilah swallowed, sadness creeping in. "Just let me grab my things, and I'll walk you out."

As they stood on the sidewalk, the hum of the city surrounding them, Delilah couldn't help but wonder what would become of them.

The next time I see you will be at a wedding," Delilah teased, trying to lighten the mood as she hugged Jobe goodbye.

"You're right." He chuckled. "I guess love is in the air this time of year."

Delilah wondered if Jobe had meant more than just Michelle, and while she was working it out, Jobe's expression changed from laughing and carefree to serious and intimate.

He took a step closer and pulled her in for a kiss.

Their lips met softly, lingering a moment longer than necessary as they savored their connection. As they broke apart, Delilah could already feel the ache of missing him.

"Safe travels, Jobe," she whispered, watching as he stepped into his taxi.

Delilah grabbed her bag and headed to work, the lingering taste of Jobe's kiss fueling her steps. The streets were alive with the pulse of the city, but Delilah found herself lost in the thoughts of Jobe and the night they had shared. He made her feel so safe and secure—someone she could truly rely on. Whenever she was with him, it was as if the whole world could disappear and as long as she had Jobe, it would be all right.

Her reverie was broken by the sudden blare of sirens, and she turned to see a firetruck speeding past. Instinctively, her mind went to Jobe—the man who had once battled flames for a living. Even though he was now a teacher, the sight of a firetruck would always remind her of him.

Then, the recent string of fires flashed through her mind, and a knot formed in her stomach. She hoped her mother was safe, unaffected by the chaos that seemed to be plaguing the city. Delilah quickened her pace, eager to lose herself in the routine of work and escape the mounting questions that swirled around her.

A GUST OF wind whipped through the half-empty parking lot as Lydia approached the designated meeting spot, her coat and purple shawl billowing behind her like a dark cape. The wind sent her hair flying around her face, her purple crystal earrings dangling in the breeze. Her heart pounded in her chest, each beat echoing the sense of urgency that had haunted her since she received Lucky B's cryptic letter.

"Lydia!" called out a voice, low and gravelly. She turned to see Lucky B leaning against the hood of his car, his sunglasses perched on top of his head despite the overcast sky.

"Thanks for coming," he said, pushing himself off the vehicle and walking toward her with a confident swagger. "I have something you need to see."

"Is it a lead?" Lydia asked, her voice steady but tinged with impatience. She didn't have time for games—people were getting hurt, and she needed answers.

"Maybe. A detective sent me this note." Lucky B handed her a folded piece of paper. As Lydia scanned its contents, her eyes widened. The nozzle she'd found at the first burned facility she'd examined matched a gas can found at a nearby facility known as the Gehenna Goods building. The address was scrawled beneath the revelation.

"Interesting," she mused, her mind racing with possibilities. "Have you checked it out?"

"Busy man," Lucky B said with a shrug, pulling his sunglasses down over his eyes. "I'll probably get to it next week. Just thought I'd let you know. Gotta run."

As he sauntered back to his car and drove off, Lydia was left standing there, clutching the note, her thoughts swirling like the wind around her.

Throughout the day, Lydia couldn't shake the nagging feeling that the Gehenna Goods building was vital to unraveling the mystery of the fires, and she decided to see if Delilah was up for an adventure. She grabbed her coat and made her way to Delilah's place. When she arrived, she told Delilah all about the building and the possible connection to the fires.

Delilah's eyes widened with excitement as Lydia described all the clues they had uncovered so far. "That definitely sounds like something worth checking out!" Delilah said enthusiastically. "Let's go! I just need to grab a few things before we head off."

Lydia smiled in relief—she was glad that she wasn't going alone. They made their way toward the mysterious building, excited yet apprehensive about what they might find there.

As the sun began to set, Lydia and Delilah arrived at their destination. The warehouse was a large, old building with dilapidated brick walls and a rusty metal roof. Many of its windows were boarded up, leaving it shrouded in darkness even though the sun lit up the sky around it.

The ominous structure stood silent and empty in the dusk, surrounded by an eerie stillness that seemed to swallow up any sound that ventured too close. As they walked closer, Lydia felt her heart beat faster in anticipation of what they might find inside; fear mingled with excitement as she wondered what secrets this place might hold. Even though there was no sign of movement around them, Lydia sensed danger lurking within this abandoned building—a feeling of angst and foreboding that only increased as they got closer to the entrance.

They exchanged a determined look before pushing open the creaky door, its hinges groaning in protest.

Once inside, the women were met with a cold, damp air permeating every corner of the Gehenna Goods building. The few windows that weren't boarded up were broken and shattered, letting in streams of muted sunset light that illuminated thick layers of dust motes suspended in the air.

The warehouse walls were crumbling and peeling, covered with remnants of past messages that had been hastily scratched out or painted over. Old boxes and crates were piled up against one side of the wall, some intact while others had been ripped apart by either time or an unknown intruder. A few cobwebs hung from the corners of the ceiling like lace curtains blowing gently in the breeze.

The further they ventured into this mysterious place, the more Lydia felt a sense of dread following them like an ominous fog. They searched every corner for clues to lead them to answers, but so far they saw nothing but old cans of paint and dusty crates covered in spiderwebs.

"Stay close," Lydia whispered, her usually calm demeanor edged with tension as they walked through the shadows.

"What do you think we'll find here, Mom?" Delilah asked, her voice a mix of excitement and apprehension.

"Answers, I hope," Lydia replied, her analytical mind already cataloging the details around them—the scattered debris, the faint scent of burnt wood lingering in the air.

As they ventured deeper into the building, Delilah suddenly gasped, seeing a coffee cup in the corner. Steam rose from the dark liquid within, indicating someone had been there recently. The realization sent a chill down Lydia's spine—perhaps they weren't alone.

"Someone was just here," Delilah murmured. "Do you think they know we're here, too?"

"Or they're still here now," said Lydia. "We need to find out what they're hiding here."

But before they could get any further, Lydia and Delilah heard a noise—faint, echoing footsteps coming from somewhere inside the warehouse.

"Did you hear that?" Lydia asked Delilah. "It sounded like footsteps."

"I think so," said Delilah.

They froze in place, their eyes darting around as they tried to detect the source of the sound. The sound was unmistakable; its heavy thuds ringing off the walls with each passing second. It sounded like someone was walking around in the darkness, and whoever it was had to know they were there.

Lydia and Delilah exchanged looks of horror before quickly retreating into the shadows to stay hidden. As they held their breath, waiting for whatever was coming their way, Lydia couldn't help but notice how loud her own heartbeats sounded against her chest. She thought she heard footsteps drawing closer and closer, yet when she paused to listen more intently, all that remained was an eerie silence that seemed to envelop them.

Soon, the noises faded away, and Lydia and Delilah found the courage to keep exploring.

With each step, Lydia couldn't help but wonder: What secrets did this place hold? And how far would they have to go to uncover the truth?

The warehouse's hollow echoes of their footsteps ceased as Lydia and Delilah finally admitted defeat, the secrets they looked for remaining stubbornly hidden.

"Okay," Delilah conceded, her breath coming out in short puffs. "We've searched everywhere, and there's nothing. Let's go before we get in trouble."

Lydia nodded, her eyes scanning the dim corners of the warehouse for any hint of a clue. But she knew her daughter was right—they had to leave. As they retraced their steps toward the entrance, Lydia's thoughts raced, her mind a whirlwind of unanswered questions and fear.

What if they'd been followed? Did someone know about their little escapade? The implications were too much to consider, and she hurried to push open the building's door, eager to leave.

"Mom, look!" Delilah hissed, grabbing Lydia's arm and pointing across the street. A green car idled there, its driver obscured by shadows but undoubtedly watching them.

"Did they see us in here?" Lydia whispered, her heart pounding.

"I don't know," Delilah replied. "But let's not stick around to find out."

As soon as the words left her mouth, the green car sped off, tires screeching against the pavement.

CHAPTER EIGHT

Lydia's heart pounded in her chest as she stared down Lucky B, the defiant tilt of his chin annoying her. "We need to identify where the arsonist will strike next and catch them red-handed," she insisted, her voice unwavering.

Lucky B had asked her to meet at his office to discuss any critical evidence she might have found, but they weren't exactly seeing eye to eye.

Lucky B scoffed, folding his arms across his broad chest. "You really think it's that easy? You can't predict when they'll strike; waiting around could be a waste of time."

"Every second we waste arguing brings us closer to another tragedy!" Lydia retorted, her usually calm demeanor giving way to frustration. Why couldn't he see how important this was?

"Look, Lydia," Lucky B said, his voice dripping with condescension, "I appreciate your enthusiasm, but you're letting your emotions cloud your judgment. Maybe it's time to step back and let us handle this. You aren't qualified to be investigating this, anyway."

Lydia's fists clenched, and her stomach did too. She knew she needed to focus on the investigation, not let his arrogance distract her. But every time she thought about another fire breaking out, she cringed at the financial impact it would have on her company—a company whose financial health was solely her responsibility. With a deep breath, she made a decision. "Fine, Lucky. You do things your way, and I'll do things mine." And with that, she stormed out of his office.

When she returned to her office, she prepared for a team meeting she had organized. She reviewed what she was going to say, reviewed her notes, and then met her colleagues in the conference room. When she entered, faces lit up, eager for the latest update about the fires. Lydia had dubbed these meetings "fire councils", and they had become a big hit at the office. The warmth of their appreciation washed over her like a balm, soothing some of the sting from her argument with Lucky B.

"Thank you all for coming," Lydia began, distributing folders filled with information about the ongoing investigation. As she detailed their progress, her colleagues nodded, impressed by her thoroughness and dedication. The fact that the nozzle she'd found was, in fact, a gas can spout that matched a container in another warehouse seemed to interest most of them.

"Hey, Lydia," an employee chimed in, his eyes sparkling with curiosity. "When's the next fire council? I don't want to miss it."

"Next week," Lydia replied, a smile creeping onto her face. "I'll make sure you're all in the loop."

After the meeting, Lydia couldn't shake the nagging feeling that Lucky B's stubbornness would hold them back from catching the arsonist. She knew she had to take matters into her own hands, even if it meant putting herself at risk.

Lydia stepped out of the conference room, her colleagues' warm smiles and appreciative nods fresh in her mind. She felt a renewed sense of purpose, the shared camaraderie refueling her determination to catch the arsonist.

"Keep up the good work, Lydia!" a colleague called as she passed by. Lydia nodded in response, grateful for the support.

Her chest tightened as she walked down the hallway, and a sudden coughing fit overtook her. Her hand flew to her mouth, trying to stifle the sound. She thought that perhaps stress from the investigation was taking its toll on her health, but she couldn't let it slow her down. Grabbing a glass of water from a nearby cooler, she took a long sip and steadied herself.

I hope I'm not overworking myself, she thought. *But I feel like I'm really close to figuring out these fires. Can't stop now.*

At home after work, Lydia settled into her favorite armchair with a cup of herbal tea. The comforting aroma of chamomile wafted around her as she pulled out a pen and a piece of paper. It was time to fill Michelle in on the latest developments.

"Dear Michelle," she wrote, her pen gliding across the paper. "We're getting closer to uncovering the truth behind these arsons. Delilah and I recently visited an abandoned warehouse that might hold the key to this mystery."

Lydia folded the letter neatly and sealed it into an envelope. Tomorrow, she would send the message to Michelle, trusting her friend's empathy and wisdom to provide the support they both needed.

As she leaned back in her armchair, Lydia considered the task before her. The stakes had never been higher, and the road ahead was uncertain and dangerous. But Lydia Boaz was no stranger to adversity, and she knew that with the support of those around her, she could overcome any challenge.

This is my chance to make a difference. I will figure this out.

With that thought echoing in her mind, she prepared for another sleepless night, her dreams haunted by the unanswered questions that lingered. And as the darkness enveloped her, Lydia steeled herself for the trials yet to come.

The next day after work, Lydia met Lucky B again to discuss the case. The sun was setting as Lydia met Lucky B in his dimly lit office. Lydia's eyes locked onto Lucky B, who leaned back in his chair, fingers interlocked and resting on his chest.

"Have you checked out the Gehenna Goods building yet?" she asked, her voice firm with determination.

Lucky B scoffed, shaking his head dismissively. "I have, but there wasn't anything of note to be found there."

"Are you sure?" Lydia pressed, her mind racing with possibilities. "Delilah and I saw something suspicious when we visited. There was someone in a green car staking out the place. It's the only lead we have."

"Trust me," he replied, his voice dripping with arrogance. "If there were anything worth finding, I would've found it."

"Regardless, I'm going back tomorrow for another look," Lydia insisted. She couldn't shake the feeling that they were missing something crucial.

"Suit yourself," Lucky B muttered, waving her off. "Sometimes evidence leads to a dead end. And that's what that building is as far as I can see."

As night fell, Lydia returned home, her thoughts racing faster than her footsteps. The memory of the stalker who had haunted her years ago resurfaced, making her tremble. She secured each lock on her doors with trembling hands, double-checking every window before retreating to her bedroom.

She lay in bed, her mind replaying the day's events, the suspicions regarding the arsonist, and the nagging uncertainty about Lucky B's motivations. As sleep eluded her, the unanswered questions swirled like smoke, threatening to choke her. Despite the mounting fear and doubt, Lydia clung to one unwavering truth: she would stop at nothing to bring the arsonist to justice.

"Whatever it takes," she whispered into the darkness, each word a promise and a prayer.

WHEN DELILAH CHECKED the mail after work, an unexpected letter was waiting for her. Her heart raced as she tore open the envelope, her hands trembling with anticipation. The familiar, elegant script on the crisp white paper sent a hint of intrigue pulsing through her, chasing away the chill of uncertainty that had consumed her in recent days. She hadn't expected to hear from Jude, but there it was—an unmistakable declaration of his feelings.

"Delilah," the letter began, "I know it has been some time since we last spoke, but I couldn't keep my thoughts and feelings hidden any longer."

As Delilah read on, Jude's words painted vivid images in her mind, memories of their shared past blooming like flowers in spring. She remembered the laughter they had shared on the bank of the Gozan River and the way his eyes sparkled when he spoke about his passion for silver coins. She had been in awe watching him walk a silver coin across his knuckles, making it disappear and then reappear like magic.

Like that coin trick, she wondered if what they shared had been real or simply an illusion.

"Perhaps we started on the wrong foot, or maybe fate conspired against us," Jude wrote. "Whatever the reason, I can't help but wonder if we could find our way back to each other."

Delilah's breath caught in her throat as she pondered the possibility. Could she really consider rekindling things with Jude? Despite everything, a part of her longed for the connection they once shared. As she folded the letter, she decided she needed a tangible reminder of those happier times.

She ventured into her storage unit, rummaging through the boxes until she found what she sought. The small table Jude had crafted for her, a crude but heartfelt gift.

Delilah carefully carried the table back to her living room, placing it in a spot where it would catch her eye every day. As she stepped back to admire it, the memories of the good times they shared came flooding back, filling her with a sense of nostalgia.

Did I give up too easily on us? she wondered, her thoughts a whirlwind of conflicting emotions. *Could we really find our way back to each other after all this time?*

Jude had always been a risky choice in Delilah's eyes, and perhaps that excited her. But it was more than that. His presence and ambition had drawn her in, and there was something mysterious about him that intrigued her. Like her wanderlust and love of travel, Jude kept her stimulated and engaged.

But the unanswered questions surrounding the arsonist investigation weighed heavily on her mind, casting a shadow over the possibility of rekindling her romance with Jude. She knew her first priority was to help her mother, Lydia, catch the arsonist and ensure their safety. The stakes were too high to be distracted by matters of the heart.

First things first, Delilah resolved, her determination returning with renewed vigor. *Once this is all over, maybe then I can explore what could have been with Jude.*

She braced herself for the challenges ahead, her heart a mixture of hope and trepidation. The path forward was uncertain, but one thing was clear—the fight for justice and love would not be won without sacrifice.

LYDIA MADE HER way to Delilah's apartment. She was nervous but determined to see if Delilah would join her in checking out the Gehenna Goods building again. She wouldn't dare involve Delilah in this if she thought it would put her in danger, but again Lydia reminded herself that arsonists targeted buildings and other objects they could burn—not people. After a few calming breaths, she knocked on the door.

Delilah opened it with a warm smile, inviting Lydia in. As soon as she stepped inside, Lydia saw that Delilah had a new table in the living room.

It was small and clearly homemade, unpolished with a rustic look to it.

"Jude made it for me," said Delilah, noting her mother's interest. "On the very bank of the Gozan River. Reminds me of home. And him."

"Ah, that was a nice gesture," said Lydia, although she never really cared for Jude. The few times she had met him didn't leave her impressed. Jobe, on the other hand, well, that was a different story.

"Well, speaking of building things," said Lydia, "do you remember how Jobe built a treehouse for you when you were kids?"

Delilah's eyes lit up. "Of course! I can still feel the rough bark of the giant oak tree he used to build it with his bare hands. He worked on it for months in secret, and then one day, he presented it to me."

Lydia smiled." You two would spend hours there, just talking and enjoying each other's company. You had all kinds of adventures."

But as Lydia looked at the table Jude had made, it was obvious that Delilah was struggling with her feelings for Jude and wanted to keep memories of their relationship alive somehow.

When Lydia finally relayed the news of what she intended to do at the Gehenna Goods building, Delilah nodded slowly. She knew how important this mission was for Lydia, and so without another word of hesitation or doubt, she agreed to go with her on their adventure.

The two women made their way to the Gehenna Goods building.

As they approached the decaying building, an eerie silence engulfed the area, broken only by the sounds of their footsteps crunching against the gravel. The warehouse loomed before them like a forgotten relic, its paint peeling away and revealing the decay beneath.

"Stay close, Delilah," Lydia said as they entered the warehouse, her voice barely above a whisper. The darkness inside the building was suffocating, pierced only by thin slivers of light streaming through the broken windows.

Delilah nodded, following her mother closely as they began to search the warehouse. Every creak and rustle sent down her spine, but she refused to let fear take hold. They needed to find any shred of evidence that could lead them to the arsonist.

"Over here!" Delilah called, her heart racing as she spotted something through a dusty window. A green car pulled up outside the warehouse—the same one they had seen watching them last time.

"Hide, now!" Lydia hissed, grabbing Delilah's arm and pulling her behind a stack of rotting boxes. They crouched down, their breaths shallow and quiet as they strained to hear any sound from outside.

"Who do you think it is?" Delilah whispered, her eyes wide with fear as she glanced at her mother. "Could it be the arsonist?"

"Shh," Lydia warned, her own heart pounding in her chest. She didn't have an answer for her daughter, but she knew whoever was in the green car posed a significant threat to their investigation—and possibly even their lives.

They huddled behind the boxes, knowing that every second spent in the warehouse increased their risk of being discovered. But they couldn't leave without finding something that could lead them closer to the truth.

Lydia hugged Delilah tightly.

From their hiding place, Lydia and Delilah could barely make out a faint knocking against the warehouse door. The sound gave her goosebumps, but they dared not move or even breathe too loudly. As the minutes dragged on, their muscles ached from crouching, but their fear anchored them firmly behind the stack of boxes.

"Mom," Delilah whispered, her voice trembling. "Do you think they're gone?"

Lydia strained to listen, her ears grasping for any hint of movement outside. When she heard nothing but silence, she finally allowed herself to exhale. "I…I think so. Let's get out of here."

Carefully, they emerged from their hiding spot and crept toward the door. Every step was calculated, their senses heightened by adrenaline. As they approached the door, however, their hearts sank. A thick chain had been looped through the handles, secured with a heavy padlock. They were trapped.

Lydia tugged at the unyielding lock. *What have I gotten us into?* "We need to find another way out!" *How could I get Delilah wrapped up in this?*

"Mom, wait…" Delilah's voice cracked as she sniffed the air. "Do you smell that?"

Lydia paused, her nostrils flaring as she detected the distinct odor of smoke. Her eyes widened in horror as they darted around the warehouse, searching for the source. "We've got to move, now!"

A plume of smoke wafted from some unknown place in the warehouse, becoming thicker and more noxious with each passing second. The smell had a dark, musky quality to it that filled the air with dread. Hazy tendrils curled around the boxes and crates, as if trying to strangle them, and Lydia could taste the smoky ash on her tongue, her eyes stinging as she tried to avert her gaze from the billowing clouds of gray and white.

CHAPTER NINE

Lydia's heart thundered in her chest as she clutched Delilah's hand, their fingers intertwined like the tendrils of smoke billowing around them. The sight of a flame danced in the distance, growing in size and intensity with each passing moment. Lydia coughed against the smoky air, her eyes widening at what she saw ahead: more flames, hungry and spreading fast.

"Mom, we need to find a way out!" Delilah's voice cracked, fear seizing her throat.

"Over there!" Lydia pointed to a shattered window, its jagged edges gleaming like teeth in the flickering light. They ran, adrenaline pumping, sweat soaking their clothes as they dodged falling debris and navigated through the choking smoke.

Lydia picked up a small plastic crate lying on the floor and scraped it around the inside edges of the window, knocking away the sharp shards of glass.

"Be careful," Lydia warned, her concern for Delilah outweighing her own fear. With a shared nod, mother and daughter squeezed through the treacherous opening, gasping as they emerged into the cool evening air.

"Are you okay?" Lydia asked, scanning Delilah for any signs of injury.

"Y-yeah, I'm fine," Delilah stuttered, shaking from the harrowing experience. "What about you?"

"Fine," Lydia confirmed, coughing harshly. Though she was sure that her eyes betrayed the simmering rage building inside her. Someone had tried to kill them, and it was personal now.

"Mom, promise me you won't do anything reckless," Delilah pleaded. But Lydia couldn't make that promise, not when their lives were in danger.

"Delilah, we almost died tonight. This person is going to pay for what they've done," Lydia vowed, determination blazing. "I have to catch them before someone else gets hurt."

"Then let me help you," Delilah insisted, squeezing her mother's hand.

"All right," Lydia relented, knowing she couldn't refuse her daughter's unwavering support. "We'll do this together."

As they stood amid the chaos, the smoke and screams of sirens filling the air, Lydia couldn't help but reflect on how close they had come to losing their lives. She was more determined than ever to find the arsonist, but the burning question remained: who were they up against?

And at that moment, as the building smoldered and crumbled behind them, Lydia knew she could not turn back. The hunt was on, and nothing would stand in her way.

DELILAH STARED AT her notebook, trying to draft the new public relations strategy for her company. Her mind kept wandering back to that harrowing night when she and her mom had barely escaped the Gehenna Goods building. She could still feel the intense heat on her skin, the choking smoke in her lungs. But here she was, alive and thriving in a job she loved.

"Delilah, these reports are fantastic!" her boss, Clarissa, exclaimed as she walked into her office. "You've really outdone yourself."

"Thank you, Clarissa," Delilah said with a grateful smile. "I didn't know if I'd hit the mark or not."

"Oh, you definitely have," Clarissa replied, her eyes softening with empathy. "Take pride in that," she added with a wink. "Value your work."

Value your work, Delilah echoed silently, another essential that was necessary for excelling at a new job. *Stay positive. Connect and communicate. Value your work.*

As much as her coworker, Tyler, had warned her about Clarissa, Delilah had found her boss to be reasonable and fair, even if she was a bit strict. It reminded Delilah not to get wrapped up in work politics, and that sometimes it was best to ignore negative comments and focus on doing a good job. That's precisely what she had done, and it had certainly paid off.

With renewed vigor, she threw herself into her work, creating innovative PR campaigns and garnering praise from Tyler and other coworkers. Her enthusiasm was infectious, and soon the entire office was buzzing with energy.

"Hey, Delilah!" called Jenia. "I heard about your latest campaign idea. It's brilliant!"

"Thanks, Jenia," Delilah responded, her cheeks flushing with pride. "I'm just trying to make a difference."

"Your passion really shows," Jenia said sincerely. "Keep up the great work!"

As Delilah continued to excel in her role, she couldn't help but feel grateful for the opportunity to make a difference—not just for her company, but for herself and her mom as well. The fire had been a terrifying ordeal, but it had ignited a fierce determination to help her mom as much as she could. It was also a reminder to be grateful for life and all of the opportunities it afforded.

Working hard is paying off, Delilah thought as she sat at her desk, reviewing the latest client feedback. *But there's so much to do.*

"Another late night?" Jenia asked as she poked his head into her office.

"Looks that way," Delilah replied, rubbing her tired eyes. "I just want to make sure everything's perfect."

"Well, don't work too hard," said Jenia. "We need you at your best, Delilah."

"Of course," she agreed, giving her a weary smile. "Thanks, Jenia."

Jenia had a point; overworking herself wasn't the way to go. Instead, she wondered if she could set challenging yet attainable goals for herself to encourage her progress. *What realistic goals can I set for myself in my early months?* It was something worth considering.

As the day finally came to an end, Delilah reflected on the progress she'd made—both professionally and in supporting her mom's mission. But as she switched off the lights and locked the office door, a nagging sense of unease crept over her. Something felt…off.

"Who is the arsonist?" she wondered aloud, her mind racing with possibilities. "And why are they doing this?"

The next day at work was a good one. Clarissa called Delilah into her office and said with a completely straight face, "I don't think I've ever promoted someone so quickly before."

"Promoted?" Delilah said, her mouth hanging open.

"You started here as a Communications Lead just a couple of months ago," said Clarissa, straight to the point as usual. "We've been without a Communications Director for a while now. I didn't know who I wanted to fill that role. With the work you've put in recently, I think you're a great fit."

Delilah was speechless. "I—I—thank you!"

Clarissa finally smiled. "Meet us in the conference room in thirty minutes so we can make it official."

Delilah beamed as she stood in front of her colleagues, her gaze fixed on the glass plaque that bore her new title: Communications Director. The gentle hum of conversation and laughter filled the room, a testament to the camaraderie that had grown among them.

"Thank you all for your support," Delilah said, with a slightly shaking voice from a mix of nerves and excitement. "I promise to keep working hard and help our company improve. And you'll be happy to know, my focus will be on improving the reach of our sales and marketing departments. I'm not sure if you're aware, but if we beat last year's numbers by just ten percent, well, there's a big bonus for you guys at the end of the year. And I want to make sure you get that!"

Everyone cheered enthusiastically.

"Couldn't have happened to a more deserving person," Jenia chimed in, beaming with pride as she clapped her hands. "You've earned this, Delilah."

"Here, here!" Tyler added, raising his glass in a toast. "To Delilah, our fearless leader!"

As they cheered, Delilah felt an overwhelming sense of gratitude for the opportunity to prove herself and make a difference. This promotion was just the beginning.

LYDIA WALKED OUT of the office building, her mind preoccupied with thoughts of the arsonist and the destruction left in their wake. As she approached her car, a figure appeared from the shadows, startling her.

"Detective Sturm," said Lydia, recognizing him with a sigh of relief. "What brings you here?"

"Ms. Boaz, just checking in to see if you know anything. Anyone you know who might be behind the fires?"

Lydia's pulse quickened, her thoughts at once going to Mitchell Irving. "Well, I do have this one employee named Mitchell Irving."

Detective Sturm pulled out a little notebook and started jotting things down.

"I found one of his business cards at the site of the first fire," Lydia went on. "Obviously, he works for the company, so it's not entirely out of the question that his business card ended up at that facility, but he works in marketing and has no reason to be at that building."

"Have you asked him about it?" asked the detective, his eyes squinting.

"Oh, definitely. He said he had no idea how it got there. But that's not all. When our Carmel center was set on fire, I saw him there watching the flames." And Lydia thought about what Jobe had told her. "I've heard that arsonists will often come back to the scene because they want to see things burn."

There was a curious gleam in the detective's eye. "That's very true. You know a lot about arsonists, don't you?"

"I'm starting to, unfortunately."

"Well, why was he there?"

Lydia ran a hand through her dark hair. "He said there was a district meeting that day with all of the marketing departments. I asked his manager, and it checked out."

Detective Sturm looked thoughtful. "Maybe he's not a suspect after all. Maybe you are."

"Me? A suspect?" Lydia's voice rose in disbelief. "You can't be serious."

The detective shrugged. "You never know who people really are. Take that arson investigator, for example, Lucky B. Well, I did some digging, and he's not exactly who he says he is."

Lydia's mouth fell open, her mind reeling with the implications of this information. Who could she trust now? "You don't think—"

"No, he's not a suspect. He just has…an interesting past, let's say that. The guy's no saint. Watch yourself."

"Thank you for telling me, Detective," she managed, her thoughts a whirlwind. "I'll keep that in mind."

As Detective Sturm retreated into the shadows, Lydia got into her car, her hands gripping the steering wheel tightly.

If Lucky B wasn't who he claimed to be, what other secrets could he be hiding?

"Who are you, Lucky B?" she murmured, her eyes narrowing. "And what do you really want?"

As Lydia drove home, she got the strange feeling that the arsonist was closer than ever—and that the truth would soon reveal itself in ways she never could have predicted.

The next day at work, Lydia couldn't shake the detective's words from her mind. She paced around her office, her thoughts consumed by Lucky B and the arson investigation. Frustration gnawed at her as she tried to make sense of it all.

Needing a break, she decided to step out for lunch, hoping the fresh air would help clear her head. As she navigated the crowded sidewalk, she accidentally bumped into Mitchell Irving.

"Sorry, Mitchell!" she apologized quickly, trying to sidestep him.

But as they collided, a lighter fell out of Mitchell's pocket, clattering onto the pavement. Lydia's eyes widened in surprise. Mitchell scooped it up hastily, avoiding eye contact.

"Uh, no problem, Lydia," he mumbled, hurrying away without another word.

Lydia stood there for a moment, watching his retreating figure, her heart pounding in her chest. The detective's words echoed in her mind: You never know who people really are.

Was Mitchell involved in the arson? Or was she just being paranoid? And what about Lucky B—who was he really?

As she returned to work, Lydia knew she couldn't ignore the growing sense of danger that surrounded her. She had to uncover the truth—and fast.

Watch yourself, the detective had warned her. And that's precisely what she intended to do.

LYDIA STOOD IN the doorway of Delilah's apartment, her thoughts ablaze from seeing Mitchell drop the lighter. The lingering smell of smoke on her clothes served as a constant reminder of their narrow escape from the burning Gehenna Goods building.

"Mom? What's wrong?" Delilah asked, the concern evident on her face.

"Can you come with me? I have a meeting with Lucky B later today, and I could use some backup," Lydia explained, her voice wavering slightly.

"Of course," Delilah agreed without hesitation, grabbing her coat. "Where are you meeting him?"

"At the park," Lydia replied. "I'd like for you to stay in the car while I talk to him. Just keep an eye on things from a distance."

Delilah nodded. "Got it."

As they drove to the park, Lydia replayed the detective's words in her mind: *He just has an interesting past.* She clenched her fists around the steering wheel, steeling herself for the meeting ahead.

They arrived at the park. Lydia parked the car and stepped out, rallying confidence.

The air was heavy and thick, with a light mist in the air. The grass was wet and muddy from where it had recently rained, the ground slick beneath her feet as she walked toward the old oak tree where Lucky B was waiting. Lydia could feel Delilah's eyes on her from a distance, comforting her with their presence. She stepped forward to meet him—unsure of what awaited ahead.

The wet autumn leaves sloshed beneath her feet as she walked toward the bench where Lucky B sat, waiting.

"Lydia," he greeted her with a grin. "Glad you could make it."

"Lucky, good to see you. What's the status of the investigation?"

"Progress is slow," Lucky B admitted, his eyes scanning the park suspiciously. "But we're following leads. Some interesting ones, in fact."

"Like what?" Lydia pressed, searching for any hints of deception in his manner.

"Can't reveal too much yet," he replied cryptically. "But I suggest keeping a close watch on your coworkers. You never know who might be involved."

"Are you implying someone I know could be the arsonist?" Lydia's heart raced, her mind flashing to Mitchell and the lighter.

"Anything's possible." Lucky B stood. Shall we walk and talk?

"Sure."

The damp earth squelched beneath Lydia's feet as she and Lucky B paced through the park, autumn leaves sticking to their shoes. The air was heavy with petrichor, a remnant of last night's storm that had drenched the city. Mud clung to the heels of Lydia's purple boots, weighing her down like the unanswered questions swirling in her mind.

"Can you at least tell me which direction your leads are pointing?" Lydia ventured, desperate for any shred of clarity.

Unfortunately, I can't," Lucky B replied coolly, his attention focused on their surroundings. "Not until I have something more concrete."

"Then at least tell me what I should be looking out for," she insisted, her frustration mounting. "I just want to protect my daughter and myself."

"Keep your eyes open and your ears sharp," he advised. "And remember—trust no one."

Lydia gritted her teeth as they continued their walk, the mud sucking at their feet with each step. She could feel

Delilah's concerned gaze from the car, watching over her like a silent guardian angel.

"Is there anything else?" asked Lucky B, stopping abruptly. His piercing gaze bore into Lydia as if seeking out her innermost thoughts.

"Nothing I can think of," she replied, trying to keep her composure. "Just… find the arsonist. Please."

"Of course," he said. "That's what I'm here for."

With that, Lucky B turned on his heel and strode away, leaving Lydia standing alone amid the mire. She watched him go, torn between relief and unease. Lydia inadvertently fumbled her notebook, sending it tumbling to the ground. Bending down to retrieve it, she caught sight of Lucky B's footprints in the mud as he left—shoe prints with a tread of little circles.

CHAPTER TEN

Delilah's heart hammered in her chest as she watched Lucky B walk away from her mother. His swagger, the way he twirled the keys around his finger—it all seemed so familiar, but she couldn't quite place him. Her mind raced through countless faces and places from her past, searching for a clue to his identity.

"Delilah!" Lydia yelled, hopping into the driver's seat. Her eyes were wide with panic, and she fumbled with the seatbelt and glanced nervously in the rearview mirror.

Delilah could tell that her mother was clearly in a state of panic, but she couldn't understand why. She had seen the look of recognition in Lydia's eyes after she bent down to pick up her notebook, but it wasn't fear—it was something else.

"Mom, what's wrong?" Delilah asked, her voice trembling. She'd never seen her mother like this before.

"Delilah," Lydia panted, "Lucky B—he's the arsonist. The shoe prints with the little circles! They were at the first three arson sites—and at one of the facilities right before it burned down!"

"Are you sure?" Delilah's stomach churned at the revelation. She knew there was something off about him, but she hadn't realized just how dangerous he really was.

"Positive," Lydia replied, gripping the steering wheel tightly as she pulled out onto the street. "We need to tell the police. We need to stop him."

"This might sound strange," said Delilah, "but I know that guy from somewhere."

"Really?" said Lydia. "It's weird because the detective working this case said Lucky B had an interesting past. He insinuated he wasn't too great of a guy and told me to be careful. But he wasn't talking about the fires; he meant something else. Something about not being who he seemed to be."

As the car sped through the city, Delilah's thoughts were consumed by the enigma that was Lucky B. If only she could remember where she'd seen him before.

Delilah thought hard. *Lucky B.* That arrogant walk, a ruthless stride. And fire. *Lucky B. Lu—Luke!* "Mom, it's Luke! Luke Belial!"

The man who had tried to bring down her father's company years ago. *The man who may have had something to do with Jobe's dad's death,* Delilah thought gravely. Her heart raced as she thought back to her time at Alexandria Meat. He'd been so smug and sure of himself, determined to make her father's meat plant go under so he could purchase the unused real estate.

She clenched her fists as they continued driving through the city streets. He was a dangerous man, and if they didn't stop him soon, who knew what else he could do? Delilah knew it wouldn't be easy to catch someone as resourceful as Luke Belial, but she also knew if anyone could do it, it was them. They were going to take Luke down.

"Who is he, Delilah?" Lydia asked, her knuckles turning white as she clutched the wheel, her eyes flicking between the road and her daughter.

"He used to work at Alexandria Meat," said Delilah. "Back when the company almost went under and I helped Dad save it. He was the one trying to get the company shut down. He's cunning and dangerous, Mom. We need to be careful."

"I remember that fiasco," said Lydia. "So he was the one behind it? And now he's wreaking havoc over here. What? Does he have a thing for our family?"

"I wonder if it's…" Delilah trailed off. "I wonder if it's revenge." *Luke hates me for sure. Probably our entire family at this point.*

As they drove on through the city, both women knew that their lives had just taken a turn down a dark and treacherous path, one from which there might be no return.

As the car sped past the neon-lit streets and bustling crowds, Delilah felt a sense of foreboding take hold of her. The world blurred around her as she focused on the man who had suddenly become their greatest adversary.

Eventually, Lydia pulled up to the curb outside of Delilah's apartment building. She turned in her seat and gave her daughter an intense look. "You need to promise me something," she said, quavering with emotion. "Promise me you won't do anything foolish. Don't go chasing after him. At least not without me. Promise me."

Delilah nodded hesitantly and gave her mother a hug before getting out of the car and waving goodbye. She watched as Lydia drove away with an uneasy feeling in the pit of her stomach, now knowing Luke was behind the recent chaos.

AS THE CAR drove away, Luke Belial smirked as he ran to get in his car. He had recognized Delilah sitting in the passenger seat as soon as he had laid eyes on her. I would know her anywhere.

He started up the engine, carefully keeping his distance so they wouldn't notice him, and followed Lydia and Delilah as they drove away. He had a feeling that this was going to be an exciting ride.

They pulled up to the front of an old brick apartment building, its façade illuminated by the street light. Luke parked across the street, keeping his eyes peeled. He watched as Delilah got out of the car and hurried inside.

The entrance was shadowed, but he could make out a dusty stairwell leading up into the building and walls painted in muted tones of gray and brown throughout, giving off a feeling of age and mystery. The hallways were dark and narrow, with peeling wallpaper in areas that seemed to have been long forgotten by time. There were several locked doors along each hallway, their metallic locks glinting in the dim light from above. Further down, there was a small garden area filled with overgrown weeds and plants that had been neglected for far too long.

Luke followed Delilah until she stopped at one door with a rusted brass knocker hanging on it. He watched as she opened the door.

He smiled. *It's so nice to know where you live, Delilah.*

LYDIA DECIDED THAT it was time to come up with a plan. She brainstormed different ideas and options, but nothing seemed to stick. Finally, as she sat in the living room of her home, an idea came to her. She could meet with Luke one last time and then follow him back to his hideout. Lydia knew this would be a risk, but if it meant stopping him from wreaking any more destruction on their city, then it was a risk worth taking.

The following day, Lydia arrived at the coffee shop on the edge of town where she and Luke had arranged to meet. She sat down across from him, and they discussed the case in hushed tones. Luke went on about not knowing who the arsonist was, and he said he should have some decent leads soon. It occurred to Lydia that, all along, these meetings had served no purpose other than letting Luke know how much she knew. *He just wanted to keep tabs on me.*

Lydia feigned interest and waited for the meeting to end. When it did, she waited until Luke got in his car, and then she quickly got into her own vehicle and started tailing him.

Lydia clenched her fists, a steely glint in her eyes, her heart pounded like a drum. She followed Luke to a small apartment building on the outskirts of the city.

As he got out of his car, Lydia was overtaken with emotion and stepped out of the shadows.

"I know who you are!" she shouted, her voice loud and full despite the tremble in her knees. Luke froze, his hand on the car door as he turned to face her. His eyes narrowed, calculating, as he assessed the situation.

"Really?" he replied, a smirk playing at the corner of his lips. "And who might that be?"

"Luke Belial," Lydia spat, venom dripping from each syllable. "And you're also the arsonist responsible for destroying lives and livelihoods across this city. It's over."

For a moment, surprise flickered across Luke's face, but it vanished just as quickly, replaced by a cold, cruel smile. He laughed, a hollow sound that echoed through the empty street. "You think you've got everything figured out, don't you? It's not that simple, Lydia."

"Simple or not, justice will be served," she retorted, her resolve unwavering. Luke studied her for a moment, his gaze piercing, before he finally responded.

"Can you prove any of this, Lydia?"

With that, he jumped into his car and sped off, tires screaming. Lydia watched him disappear around a corner, her heart pounding, and she scrambled into her own car to follow.

Lydia's tires screeched as she slammed on the accelerator, tearing after Luke's retreating car. Adrenaline flooded her veins as she sped after him through the city streets. The wind whipped through her hair, the smell of exhaust and burning rubber filling her nostrils.

Through the crowded streets, she wove between cars like a needle threading fabric. Pedestrians dove out of the way, their screams barely audible over the roaring engines. Lydia could see Luke's taillights flicker up ahead, growing smaller with each passing second.

Lydia knew that if she took a shortcut through the alleyway a few blocks away, she might be able to cut him off. It was risky, but she had no other choice.

As the car rocketed through the narrow passage, Lydia's eyes darted between the brick walls and the rearview mirror, gauging the distance between her and Luke. He was ahead by a few car lengths, but she was gaining ground.

"Almost there…almost there," Lydia whispered, her focus unwavering.

Luke suddenly swerved onto a side street, his tires squealing in protest. Lydia followed suit, her tires skidding against the pavement as she pushed the car to its limit. They raced through a busy intersection, narrowly avoiding collisions with oncoming traffic.

Up ahead, Luke's car was now only a car length away. Lydia could see the panic in his eyes as he glanced in the rearview mirror, realizing that she was closing in. He gunned the engine, desperate to escape, but Lydia refused to be shaken.

Luke Belial, you won't get away from me.

As they barreled down the city streets, Lydia called upon every ounce of focus she could muster. She knew the city like the back of her hand, using her intimate knowledge of its twists and turns to gain ground on Luke.

"Almost got you," Lydia murmured, her heart racing as she felt the thrill of the chase surge through her.

All that mattered was catching Luke before he vanished into the labyrinth of the city.

Lydia swerved around a delivery truck, the wheels of her car screeching. Luke's vehicle was just a hair's breadth ahead of her, weaving in and out of traffic with reckless abandon.

CHAPTER TEN

A pedestrian darted across the street, and Lydia slammed on the brakes, narrowly avoiding a collision. Her knuckles turned white on the steering wheel, and she muttered a silent prayer for the safety of those around them.

"You won't get away!" Lydia hissed through clenched teeth. As they raced past a bustling market, she saw her chance—an alleyway shortcut that would bring her closer to Luke. She veered off the main road and navigated the narrow passage.

As she emerged from the alley, Lydia's heart leaped into her throat. Luke's car was only a few feet away now, but their path was blocked by construction equipment. With no time to waste, she jerked the wheel to the right, skidding around the obstacle and onto another busy street.

I can't let him slip through my fingers.

Barely missing a cyclist, Lydia gritted her teeth and pressed her foot down hard on the accelerator. Ahead, Luke swerved around a parked car and careened down a side street. Lydia followed in hot pursuit, her determination fueled by adrenaline and the knowledge that she was closing in on him.

"Almost there," she murmured, her breath coming in short, ragged gasps. "Just a little closer…"

As they rounded another bend, Lydia's heart sank. The street ahead was teeming with people, a colorful parade weaving its way through the city. She slammed on the brakes, skidding to a halt just inches from the celebratory crowd.

He's getting away! Her eyes scanned rapidly for any sign of Luke. And then she saw it—a flash of his red taillights disappearing down a side street. She shifted gears and plunged into the fray, her eyes locked on her target.

Luke, I'm coming for you.

Luke's car swerved into a narrow alley, tires screaming against the asphalt. Lydia gritted her teeth, yanking the wheel to follow him, her heart pounding in her chest.

He's going to lose me! Lydia nearly panicked at the thought as she navigated the labyrinth of narrow streets and dark corners.

"Not today," Lydia growled. Failure was not an option.

The cityscape blurred around her, a discord of honking horns and shouting pedestrians. The scent of grilled street food mingled with exhaust fumes, assaulting their senses as they tore through the city. Luke's taillights flickered like a sinister beacon, always just a little too far ahead for comfort.

Luke took a sudden turn onto a one-way street, forcing Lydia to take another route.

But Lydia refused to give up, her gaze hardening in resolve as she steered the car through an unfamiliar section of town. In the distance, she could make out Luke's taillights, bobbing in and out of view like a beacon in the night.

Closer. Faster. Lydia's grip tightened on the wheel as her car raced down the narrow city streets. She could feel her heart pounding in her chest, the adrenaline fueling her determination.

"You can't run forever," she whispered, beads of sweat forming on her brow.

Luke swerved left. Lydia followed, her eyes never leaving his car. The distance between them was shrinking. She was so close now she felt like she could reach out and touch him.

The chase led them into a maze of alleys, each turn more treacherous than the last. Luke's desperation was evident in the erratic movements of his vehicle as he tried to shake her off his tail. But Lydia refused to relent, her unwavering focus driving her forward.

"Your time is running out, Luke," she muttered.

She floored the accelerator, her eyes never leaving the red lights ahead of them. She edged closer and closer until she was so close that she could almost taste victory. So close.

With a deafening screech, Lucky's car skidded to a stop in front of a dead end. Lydia slammed on her brakes, bringing her car to an abrupt halt just inches from his bumper.

Game over. She climbed out of the car. Her stomach clenched as her gaze met Luke Belial's.

With no place left to run, Luke leaped from his car, scrambling over a tall fence to escape.

Lydia bolted from the car and peered into Lucky B's abandoned vehicle.

Nestled among the debris of his hurried flight lay a small note on the seat. Lydia read it and gasped. *"I have your daughter."*

CHAPTER ELEVEN

Luke's pulse quickened as he paced the dimly lit room, his eyes resting on Delilah, bound to an old wooden chair. *Revenge is sweet.*

Delilah had been the single reason for his unsuccessful acquisition of the real estate of Alexandria Meat two years ago. He'd had a nearly perfect plan, sowing dissension at the meat plant and causing the company's production to be affected. Just when the company was about to go under, Delilah united the employees and exposed him. She had done so with the help of her father, Abe, and so it only seemed right that he took revenge on Delilah and her mother, Lydia. Since they both worked for the meat industry in New York, it had been a two-for-one deal—two birds with the same well-placed stone.

While the first two warehouse fires that happened before Lydia started working for New York Meat had been accidents, it had given him the idea for the perfect vehicle of reprisal when he found out about Lydia's new job.

He had stood to make a lot of money from buying the Alexandria Meat building, but the Boaz family had put an end to that. He hated them.

But now, the tables had turned. He'd wreaked havoc on the meat plants in New York, causing both Delilah and Lydia stress and misfortune. And now he held Delilah captive, and he would make sure she nor her mother could ever get in his way again. He would bring the Boaz family to its knees.

The revelations that Delilah and Lydia had uncovered threatened to undo everything he'd worked so hard for. He had lied to Lydia—and everyone else—in the very beginning, telling them the first two fires weren't accidents, when, in fact, they had been. If everyone knew they were unintentional, they would investigate the company's machinery and practices. The fact was, New York Meat was using old equipment that needed to be replaced. The machines had overheated and started fires—but if the company knew that, they would've corrected the problem. And that's not what he wanted. He wanted Lydia to suffer as much as possible, and as CFO, what would hurt her more than company buildings burning down and incurring massive profit losses?

He had also planted Mitchell Irving's business card at an arson site to cause Lydia to suspect him, and he'd even sent Lydia an anonymous warning not to get involved in the arson investigation. And, of course, he had planted that gas can nozzle near one of the earlier burned-down warehouses just to throw Lydia off. But they had figured it out anyway somehow. If they got him arrested, the Boaz family would win again—and he'd lose his freedom. In his mind, there was only one solution—both women had to be eliminated.

I'm going to put an end to this. He knew Lydia wouldn't just let her daughter vanish without a fight; she was too much of an obstacle to leave unchecked. She needed to be dealt with, and if he could lure her here to this old warehouse where her daughter lay bound, he could take them both out at once.

With a sinister smile, Luke decided to turn the structure into a deathtrap for Delilah and Lydia.

The warehouse loomed before him, its skeletal frame casting ominous shadows on the cracked concrete floor. Luke moved quickly, planting explosives along the walkways, in the corners, and in various other strategic locations throughout the building. His fingers trembled with anticipation as he set the timers, all the while imagining the look of terror on Lydia's face when she realized her doom.

"Tick-tock, Lydia," he whispered, holding the detonator tightly in his hand. "Your time is running out."

As he surveyed his handiwork, Luke couldn't help but indulge in a moment of self-congratulation.

His trap was perfect; once Lydia was inside, she had no chance of escape. He'd be able to eliminate them both at the same time. He allowed himself a satisfied smirk as he prepared to leave the warehouse, now filled with enough explosives to create a deadly explosion.

Luke had done his job well—he had crafted an intricate web of death that even the most agile of foes could not hope to escape from. He knew whatever happened now, his plan was foolproof; no matter who entered this place or what their intentions were, he was certain that they wouldn't make it out alive.

This was his masterpiece, a symphony of destruction that would rid him of Lydia *and* Delilah once and for all. But deep down, something gnawed at him. Was it guilt? Regret? No, those emotions were for the weak. Luke Belial had no room for such sentiments in his heart. This was merely a necessity, he told himself, just something that had to be done. *I've come too far to question myself now.*

With the warehouse transformed into an explosive deathtrap, all that remained was for Lydia to take the bait. Luke could hardly contain his anticipation—soon, the family who had wronged him would be decimated.

"Let the games begin," Luke said, a wicked grin spreading across his face as he clutched the detonator close to his chest. It wouldn't be long now.

LYDIA'S HEART POUNDED in her chest, the blood rushing through her ears as she stared at the note Luke had left. Every fiber of her being screamed in agony at the thought of Delilah in danger. Her world seemed to collapse around her, and she could feel the walls closing in.

"Delilah," she whispered, tears spilling down her face. "I'll find you, I promise."

She couldn't waste a moment. Racing out of her apartment, Lydia went straight to the police station, her mind racing with thoughts of what Luke might do to her daughter.

"Officer, my daughter has been kidnapped!" she exclaimed, thrusting the note into the hands of the nearest officer. "Please, you have to help me find her!"

"Ma'am, we'll do everything we can," the officer assured her, but Lydia knew she couldn't just sit by idly. Time was precious, and she had to take matters into her own hands.

"Detective Sturm, I need your help," Lydia said, barging into his office without so much as a knock. "Luke has taken Delilah, and God only knows what he's planning."

Detective Sturm looked puzzled. "Luke? Who's—"

"Lucky B," Lydia blurted. "His real name is Luke Belial."

A look of knowing passed over the detective's face, and he made a fist with his right hand and rested his chin on it.

"That's right. When I looked up his background, I saw his real name was Luke Belial." He squinted his eyes. "But how do you know that?"

Lydia told Detective Sturm everything.

"Lydia, slow down," Detective Sturm said, his voice steady and calm. "We'll find her, but we need to think rationally. Where could he have taken her?"

"Anywhere," Lydia replied, her mind spinning as she thought of all the places they had explored while investigating Luke. "The arson sites, the Gehenna Goods building we visited before… even his apartment."

"All right," said Sturm, grabbing his coat and following Lydia out the door.

As they raced from location to location, Lydia's desperation grew. At each site, she found nothing—no sign of Delilah or Luke. Her heart ached with each fruitless search, but she refused to give up.

"His apartment," Lydia said, hoarse from the panic and fear that had consumed her. "We have to check there."

"Lydia, I know you're scared," Detective Sturm said, placing a hand on her shoulder. "But we can't let our emotions cloud our judgment. Let's approach this carefully."

"Every second we waste is another second Delilah could be in danger," Lydia snapped, her eyes blazing with determination. "I won't let anything happen to her."

With Detective Sturm's help, they gained access to Luke's apartment, but it was empty. The crushing weight of despair settled on Lydia's shoulders, but she couldn't let it consume her. She had to keep searching, keep fighting for her daughter.

"Where are you, Delilah?" she whispered, feeling more lost and helpless than ever before.

As they left the apartment, Lydia's mind raced. Where could Delilah be? What were Luke's plans? And most importantly, how could she save her daughter before it was too late?

"He's probably watching you," said Detective Sturm. "If he has your daughter, he's likely using her as bait to get you too. I'll be posted outside your place in an unmarked car this evening. If anything happens, I'll be close."

Lydia thanked Detective Sturm and made her way home. She could hardly breathe, wondering if her daughter was all right. As the hours passed, it killed her to think there was nothing she could do. She felt guiltier than she ever had, in the comfort of her own home while Delilah had been kidnapped and was suffering some unknown fate.

She gazed sadly out of her window, and Lydia's heart pounded as she spotted the familiar green car lurking outside her apartment. This was her chance—the lead she so desperately needed to find Delilah. Knowing that Detective Sturm was out there as well made things even better. She hurried down to her own car, her hands shaking as she fumbled with the keys. The moment she started the engine, the green car pulled away. Lydia followed, keeping a safe distance to avoid detection.

She hoped Detective Sturm was following too.

"Please, let this be it," she whispered. "Please let me find Delilah."

The green car led her through the city and eventually to another abandoned warehouse. Lydia's pulse quickened as she watched Luke exit the vehicle and stride confidently inside. This had to be where he was holding Delilah. He had obviously led her there, so Lydia thought it might be a good idea to scope the place out before she rushed inside. When she drove around to the back of the building, she found the rear door left open with a chain and lock hanging loose.

She secured the lock and returned to the front entrance. *You won't be escaping that way, Luke.*

Lydia pulled her car back around to the front of the building.

As Lydia crept inside, the musty smell of decay assaulted her senses. The dim light filtering through the grime-coated windows revealed towering stacks of wooden crates and narrow walkways between them. The air was thick with dust, making it difficult to breathe. But she pushed on, determined to save her daughter from Luke's sinister grasp.

"Delilah!" Lydia called out, her voice echoing through the cavernous space. "Where are you?"

Her footsteps echoed on the concrete floor as she navigated the labyrinth of crates and passages. Each creak and groan of the old building sent a cold tremble through her, but she refused to let fear paralyze her.

"Think, Lydia, think," she muttered to herself. "What would he do? Where would he hide her?"

Desperation fueled her every step, the minutes ticking away like a countdown. She knew the longer Delilah was in Luke's clutches, the more dangerous the situation became. The stakes were higher than ever, and there was no room for mistakes.

"Mom!" a distant voice cried out, barely audible over the sound of Lydia's own heartbeat.

"Delilah!" she shouted back, sprinting toward the source of the voice. "I'm coming!"

As she raced through the warehouse, Lydia's mind whirred with plans, questions, and fears. But one thing was clear: she would not stop until her daughter was safe in her arms again. And when that moment came, they would face the consequences together.

Stay strong, Delilah, Lydia thought, her eyes brimming with tears. *We will overcome this. We have to.*

Lydia's heart pounded as she darted through the dimly lit warehouse, her eyes straining to catch a glimpse of Luke slipping away into the shadows. He was like a specter, there one moment and gone the next. But she couldn't let him escape; Delilah's life depended on it.

"Delilah!" Lydia yelled again, her voice echoing off the cold metal walls. No response—only the eerie silence that seemed to swallow her calls whole.

A faint clanging sound rang out above her, drawing her attention to the catwalk that crisscrossed overhead like a spider's web. Without hesitation, Lydia sprinted toward the nearest access point, her determination leaving no room for fear or doubt.

"Where are you?" she whispered under her breath, her eyes scanning the maze-like walkways in search of her daughter—or any sign of her captor.

IN THE SHADOWS, Luke grinned maliciously as he tapped his fingers against the metal railing, creating a symphony of dissonant sounds that echoed throughout the warehouse. He knew Lydia would be unable to resist following the noise, luring her further into his trap.

Keep coming, Lydia, he thought to himself, the corners of his lips curling up in anticipation. *Soon, it'll all be over.*

He could see her ascend the walkway.

"Delilah!" Lydia cried, her voice breaking with desperation.

She raced along the walkways, screaming.

"Luke! You won't get away with this!"

Luke laughed coldly. "Come find me, Lydia!" he called, his voice dripping with malice. "I'm waiting."

He faded into the darkness, quieting his footsteps as he circled back around to the front door of the warehouse. He moved with the grace and stealth of a predator, knowing every twist and turn of this forsaken place. Reaching the front entrance, he quickly locked it with a chain and padlock around the handles, sealing Lydia and Delilah inside.

"Time for the grand finale," he murmured, his eyes gleaming with sinister delight.

Luke's fingers brushed against the detonator in his pocket, and he relished the device's cold metal against his skin. As he made his way toward the back door, his mind raced with thoughts of the destruction that would soon follow, and the satisfaction of his victory over Lydia. The rush and excitement of it all drowned out any lingering doubt or remorse.

Once I push this button, it's all over, he thought, the power of life and death resting in his hands.

With the exit just steps away, Luke pressed the detonator. The warehouse erupted with a series of deafening explosions, shattering the silence and shaking the floor beneath his feet. The sounds of crashing and crumbling filled the air as the once-imposing structure began to collapse in on itself.

"YES!" Luke shouted, laughing maniacally as he reveled in the chaos he'd created. The flames leaped and danced around him, casting eerie shadows on the walls. For a moment, he felt like a god, commanding the elements themselves.

But as he reached for the back door, his triumphant expression faltered. The handle wouldn't budge. It was locked from the outside.

LYDIA'S HEART HAMMERED in her chest as she sprinted through the burning warehouse, each breath a searing pain in her throat. The explosion had sent debris flying everywhere, and now flames licked hungrily at the walls, filling the air with biting smoke. Her vision wavered, but she knew she couldn't afford to hesitate, not with Delilah inside.

"Delilah!" she cried, her voice barely rising above the roar of the fire. "Where are you?"

As Lydia rounded a corner, she spotted a small room amid the chaos, its door hanging crooked on its hinges. Inside, she found Delilah bound to a chair, fear lined deep into her face.

"Mom!" Delilah exclaimed, relief washing over her features.

Lydia wasted no time untying her daughter's bindings. "We need to get out of here," she said urgently, gripping Delilah's hand in her own.

"Luke...he's—" Delilah began, coughing from the smoke.

"Let's focus on getting out first," Lydia interjected, guiding Delilah through the hellish landscape. They scrambled over fallen beams and navigated around collapsed walkways, the heat singing their skin.

Outside, sirens wailed and tires screeched as emergency vehicles pulled into the building's parking lot. A flicker of hope ignited within Lydia—her plan was working. But they needed to escape before the building crumbled around them.

"Up here!" Lydia shouted, pulling Delilah toward a narrow staircase that led upwards. As they climbed, the smoke grew thicker, making it nearly impossible to see. But Lydia pushed on, desperation fueling her every step.

Finally, they stumbled onto the roof, gasping for air. Below, cop cars and a fire truck swarmed the parking lot, Detective Sturm among them.

"Over there, a fire escape ladder!" Delilah pointed, her voice hoarse from the smoke.

"Come on, we can make it!" Lydia encouraged, and they raced across the roof, the heat radiating through their shoes. They reached the ladder just as the warehouse groaned ominously behind them.

"Go, go, go!" Lydia urged, practically shoving Delilah onto the ladder first. She followed quickly, her heart throbbing as they descended toward safety.

As they reached the ground, Lydia's legs nearly buckled beneath her, but she managed to stay upright, supporting

Delilah as they both stumbled toward Detective Sturm and the other emergency personnel.

"Mom…we made it," Delilah whispered, tears streaming down her face.

"We did," Lydia agreed, wrapping her arms around her daughter, grateful to have escaped with their lives.

The sound of shattering glass echoed through the air, drawing everyone's attention to the warehouse. Luke barreled out of a broken window, a storm of shards and embers following him like a vengeful cloud. He crashed onto the ground, coughing violently as he tried to breathe.

"Luke!" Lydia shouted, her voice strained with a mixture of anger and disbelief. She hadn't expected him to make it out alive, let alone so dramatically.

Luke rolled onto his back, slowly coming to a stop. He lay there for a few seconds, his clothes charred and his face smeared with soot. His breathing ragged and labored, he shakily got to his feet, broken glass radiating from the floor beneath him like a glittering constellation.

He looked around him, surveying the scene of police officers, detectives, and emergency personnel that had formed in the parking lot. His gaze finally settled on Lydia and Delilah standing nearby, their faces illuminated by the orange firelight and the pulsing blue lights of police cars.

Luke stumbled forward, his feet unsteady from the fall. He fixed Lydia with a glare, as though daring her to act against him. But before she could even move, he tripped over his feet and fell to the ground, coughing.

CHAPTER TWELVE

Luke's face contorted in pain and rage, and Lydia stepped forward.

"Everyone, this is the arsonist!" Lydia shouted. "His name is Luke Belial!"

Luke's eyes flickered with surprise and fear for a moment before he regained his composure. The detonator, clutched in his hand, fell to the ground with a metallic clatter as he staggered to his feet.

"Who do you think you are, accusing me like that?" he snarled, sweat beading on his forehead, betraying his nerves.

"Admit it, Luke," Lydia demanded, her gaze meeting his without flinching. "You're responsible for all those fires, for all the pain and suffering you've caused."

"Fine! You want the truth? I did it!" Luke screamed, all pretense of innocence gone. He looked down at the detonator he'd dropped, as if knowing he could no longer deny his involvement. "And I would've gotten away with it too if it weren't for you! "

Lydia's mind raced as she tried to process what was happening. This man who had terrorized their community stood before them: cornered, angry, and dangerously unpredictable.

Detective Sturm ran up, several officers at his sides. They surrounded Luke, guns aimed and ready.

"Luke Belial, you're under arrest for arson and attempted murder!" Detective Sturm declared.

Relief washed over Lydia as the police handcuffed Luke and led him away. Lydia turned to her daughter, tears glistening.

"Thank God we're safe," Lydia whispered, pulling Delilah into a tight embrace. Lydia's thoughts swirled, her emotions a chaotic storm as she hugged her daughter.

LUKE'S VISION BLURRED as the police officer shoved him into the back seat of the patrol car. His head throbbed, a vicious drumbeat that matched the relentless pace of his racing heart. The cold steel of the handcuffs dug into his wrists, causing him to wince in pain. How could he have been so careless?

"Stupid," he muttered to himself, gritting his teeth. "You should've seen it coming."

The car lurched forward, and Luke's stomach churned with each twist and turn through the city streets. He stared

ference room, the air was electric with anticipation. They all knew the significance of this meeting—that their nightmare was finally behind them. It was so important that their CEO was in attendance.

"Thank you all for being here," Lydia began, her voice clear and full. "As you know, we've finally apprehended the arsonist responsible for the fires at our facilities. I want to express my deepest gratitude for your unwavering support and cooperation during this difficult time."

There was a round of earnest applause, and Lydia continued. "I'd like to propose an idea to our CEO, Rico Lane, to commemorate our resilience. I want to commission a local artist to paint a mural at one of the arson sites—a phoenix rising from the ashes. I suggest our Nod Warehouse, since the damage there was far less than at the other sites, and it will be up and running the soonest."

The room buzzed with excitement as the employees exchanged enthusiastic glances. Lydia could feel the energy shift in the room, a sense of hope and unity washing over them all.

"Lydia, I think it's a fantastic idea, and I fully approve of the project," Rico confirmed, his gaze intense and supportive.

"Thank you, Rico," Lydia said, her heart swelling with pride. The meeting adjourned on a high note, leaving everyone with a renewed sense of purpose.

A week later, Lydia made her way to the partially burned Nod Warehouse where the mural was to be painted.

As she approached, she could see the artist, perched on a scaffold, already hard at work on the unscathed side wall. The sound of the brush against the wall was rhythmic and calming, like a heartbeat.

Lydia stood back, watching as the phoenix took shape on the once-charred wall. Fiery shades of red and orange blended seamlessly, creating a mesmerizing illusion of flames dancing around the mythical creature. The trace of fresh paint hung in the air, mingling with the lingering smell of ash and soot—a testament to the fire that had ravaged the building not long ago.

It's beautiful.

Lydia felt a sense of awe at the transformation taking place before her eyes. It was as if the phoenix symbolized their own rise from the ashes, a testament to their strength and resilience.

DELILAH ENTERED HER office, the familiar scent of coffee and paper filling her nostrils. She had missed this place while dealing with the harrowing ordeal that nearly cost her and her mother their lives. As she approached her desk, she noticed a banner hanging from the ceiling—"Welcome Back, Delilah!"

"Hey, Delilah!" her coworker Tyler called as he appeared in the doorway. "We heard about what happened. You know, with the arsonist. I'm glad you're okay."

"Thank you, Tyler," Delilah replied, her voice wavering slightly. "It was…quite an experience."

Her other coworker, Priya, joined them, her arms laden with party decorations. "We're throwing you a little work party to celebrate your return and show how happy we are that you're safe," she announced.

"Really, guys? You didn't have to do that," Delilah said, touched by their thoughtfulness.

"Of course, we did," Jenia insisted, placing a hand on Delilah's shoulder. "You're family to us, and we want you to know that we're here for you."

As the impromptu celebration unfolded around her, Delilah couldn't help but feel grateful for the support of her colleagues. She knew it would take time to heal from the trauma, but being surrounded by friends made the process a little easier.

AT HOME LATER that evening, Delilah sat at her kitchen table, pen in hand and a blank piece of paper in front of her. Michelle's wedding was fast approaching, and as the maid of honor, Delilah had been tasked with writing a speech. She wanted it to be perfect—a testament to their friendship and the many memories they'd shared over the years.

Her mind wandered to their teenage years, finding themselves in the small town of Alexandria and the nearby city, Mount Moriah. She recalled the summer days spent swimming in the Gozan River, the sun warm on their skin as they splashed and laughed in the water. The aroma of wildflowers filled the air around them, a sweet perfume that seemed to linger even after they had left the riverbank.

Delilah remembered the picnics they'd had along the banks, feasting on sandwiches and fruit as they shared stories and dreams. She remembered fun evenings at O'Malley's Irish pub, and dancing at night to the light of glowing fireflies. The taste of homemade lemonade lingered on her tongue, a bittersweet reminder of simpler times.

But it wasn't just the good days Delilah remembered, but the tough times too. She keenly recalled the fire at Michelle's art studio several years ago, where the building had been set ablaze while they were still inside—another fire Luke had been responsible for. It was one of the most frightening experiences of her life, but she could get through anything with Michelle by her side.

With that memory in mind,

As the memories continued to flow, Delilah's pen began to dance across the paper, bringing to life the stories of two emerging young ladies discovering the world. She knew no matter what challenges life threw at them, she and Michelle would always have each other's backs.

With a sigh, Delilah set down her pen, her eyes scanning the words she had written. The speech was a tribute to the bond she and Michelle shared, a reflection of their love and friendship. And as she reread the final lines, Delilah wondered what other challenges life might throw their way.

It didn't matter, she realized, as long as they had each other.

"DELILAH, ARE YOU ready? We have a lot of dresses to try on!" Lydia called from the living room.

Delilah glanced at her reflection in the mirror one last time before joining her mother. They left Delilah's apartment, hopped into Lydia's car, and drove to the bridal shop.

"Let's find the perfect dress for Michelle's wedding," Delilah said excitedly. As they entered the boutique, a whirlwind of colors and fabrics greeted them. A saleswoman approached with a welcoming smile.

"Welcome, ladies! Are you looking for something specific?" she asked, her eyes scanning their faces for clues.

"We're here to find a bridesmaid dress for this lovely young lady," Lydia replied, gesturing proudly to Delilah. "The color is lilac."

"Oh, beautiful!" the saleswoman replied. "Yeah, lilac and lavender are really in right now, and they're such nice colors! Let me show you our selection." She led them through the maze of delicate gowns, each one more beautiful than the last.

Delilah slipped into the first gown, the silk fabric whispering against her skin as she spun around to face her mother. "What do you think?"

"Beautiful," Lydia said, her eyes filling with pride. "But let's keep looking. We want to find the perfect match for Michelle's theme."

They continued trying on dresses, the beauty of the garments eliciting gasps of awe from both women. They narrowed it down to two dresses: one that was strapless with a corset-style top; and another one that started off formfitting but became more flowy as it cascaded down past the ankles.

"What do you think, Mom," Delilah asked, spinning slow circles in the flowy dress with the long hem. She gazed at herself in the mirror.

"They're both so nice!" said Lydia, her hands clasped together. Then her eyes drifted to the strapless dress draped over the changing room door. "Okay, try the strapless one on just one more time!"

Delilah laughed and went back into the changing room. She came out and modeled the dress for Lydia—and checked herself out in the mirror a few more times. She loved how the lack of straps accentuated her neck and shoulders.

"I think that's the one, honey," said Lydia. "Your neck and shoulders look so good without any straps—"

"I was just thinking the same thing!" Delilah interrupted.

Lydia clapped. "We've decided on a dress!"

But as Delilah looked at herself in the mirror, she felt something was missing.

"Mom, I need a change," Delilah declared, her voice.

Lydia raised an eyebrow. "You're talking about your hair, aren't you?"

Delilah laughed. "You know me too well." She ran her fingers through her platinum blonde hair. "Yeah, I think it's about time."

"Are you sure, sweetheart?" Lydia asked, concern etched on her face. "The platinum blonde was a big hit."

"It definitely was, but I want to try something new. Something more subdued, like a dark brunette."

With Lydia's support, Delilah found herself seated in a stylist's chair the very next day. As the stylist carefully applied the dye to her hair, Delilah felt a thrill of anticipation.

"Ready or not, here it comes!" the stylist said excitedly.

"Oh, I'm ready!" Delilah replied confidently, feeling a renewed sense of adventure.

As the last strand of hair was trimmed, Delilah looked at her reflection and gasped. The brunette locks framed her face perfectly, giving her an air of sophistication and mystery. She knew she had made the right decision.

"Thank you," she whispered, her fingers running through the soft strands. "This is exactly what I needed."

As Delilah left the salon, she thought back on all the events that had led her to this moment—the danger they'd faced, the strength she'd discovered within herself, and the unbreakable bond she shared with her loved ones. As she walked out into the bustling city, a newfound sense of purpose filled her heart, knowing there were challenges to overcome and secrets waiting to be uncovered. But whatever lay ahead, she was ready to face it, armed with the love and support of those who mattered most.

Delilah stepped outside, the sun high in the sky casting a warm glow on her newly dyed brunette hair. Honking horns and lively chatter filled the air as she made her way down the crowded sidewalk, a crush of people surrounding her. The scent of street food wafted through the air, a tantalizing blend of sizzling hot dogs, caramelized onions, and freshly baked pretzels.

"Hey, lady, watch it!" a cyclist shouted, nearly clipping Delilah as she crossed the street. She muttered an apology under her breath, eyes scanning the cityscape, taking in the towering skyscrapers and bustling storefronts.

As she strolled through the city, Delilah couldn't help but marvel at its energy, the unrelenting pace both exhilarating and exhausting. The laughter of children playing in a nearby park mingled with the rhythmic beat of a street performer's drums, creating a symphony of sound that was uniquely New York.

Remember what Dad used to say about this city? Delilah thought, a nostalgic smile tugging at her lips. Something about a million stories unfolding all at once."

Delilah headed home as the sun began its decline.

The thought of her father fresh in her mind, Delilah decided to make his favorite dish for dinner: grilled lamb chops.

The aroma of searing meat filled her apartment, the sizzle of the chops on the hot pan a comforting soundtrack to her evening. She took a moment to appreciate the simple pleasure of preparing a meal, a small but meaningful connection to her father. As she savored each tender bite, Delilah thought fondly of the countless meals she'd shared with her dad, his large presence echoing in her memories. She couldn't help but wonder what he was up to.

She finished her meal and gazed out at the city skyline.

The sun was setting, casting a muted glow over Delilah's apartment as she cleared away the remnants of her meal. Her thoughts lingered on her father, but also on the mail that was waiting for her attention. She made her way to the small stack of envelopes, fingers already anticipating the familiar texture of paper.

"Jude," she whispered, recognizing the handwriting on an envelope.

Another letter from Jude.

Delilah was sure that this letter would be like the last one she received, Jude expressing his interest in getting back together. And it was. It certainly was. But that didn't mean she was prepared for the sentence she just read.

It shocked her.

CHAPTER THIRTEEN

Delilah's hands trembled as she unfolded the letter. Jude's familiar handwriting stared back at her, a heartbeat away from leaping off the page.

"I'm saddened that you haven't responded to my letter and that we can't be together again. Is it because of Jobe?"

The words struck like a bolt of lightning. Her heart raced as images of Jobe filled her mind—his gentle smile, his warm eyes, the way he always seemed to know exactly what to say. She set the letter down on the small table Jude had made for her years ago. A symbol of their commitment now twisted into a reminder of the confusion tearing at her heart.

Is it because of Jobe? The question echoed in her mind, refusing to be silenced. *Was she hesitant about giving Jude another chance because Jobe was still in her heart?*

Delilah pushed these thoughts aside. This wasn't the time to dwell on her crumbling love life. Her mother would be there soon, and they had a flight to catch. Michelle's wedding was only days away.

Lydia arrived, and the two took a taxi to the airport. After a whirlwind of suitcases and tickets, Delilah found herself seated next to her mother on the plane bound for Mount Moriah. She couldn't wait to be home; she hadn't seen her father, Abe, in months. The thought brought a rush of emotions, each battling for dominance.

"I'm so excited for Michelle's wedding!" said Lydia.

Delilah wondered if her mother could sense her inner turmoil. "Me too," she said, forcing a smile. "It's been a long time since we've all been together. It'll be so good to see Dad again."

With a longing smile, Delilah thought about her father—his warmth and kindness, his firmness when it was needed. He had always guided her and pushed her to be her very best, and she was grateful for it. It had molded her into the woman she is today: kind, bold, and adventurous.

Several hours later, as the plane began its descent into Mount Moriah, Delilah couldn't help but wonder if seeing Jobe would provide the answers she yearned for. Would her heart finally decide between Jude and Jobe?

The wedding was fast approaching, and Delilah knew that seeing Abe and Michelle would provide a much-needed distraction from the war raging within her. She clung to the hope that being surrounded by love and happiness would guide her to the right path.

Lydia touched her arm gently. "Are you okay?"

"Of course," Delilah said, forcing another smile. "Just thinking about everything."

"Take it one step at a time, honey," Lydia advised. "You'll figure it out."

As the plane landed on Mount Moriah's soil, Delilah felt the unanswered questions bearing down on her. The upcoming reunion with her father, Abe, and Michelle's wedding loomed large in her mind. But beneath it all, the thought of seeing Jobe again burned like an ember, threatening to ignite her world into chaos all over again.

THE SUN WAS setting as Delilah, Lydia, and Abe gathered around the dining table in Abe's comfortable home. The vibrant orange and red hues of the sunset streamed through the window, casting a warm glow on their faces. Laughter filled the room as they reminisced about old times, the tension from the plane ride all but forgotten.

Although Abe and Lydia had divorced twelve years ago, they had always been friendly, and they were able to enjoy these moments of merriment as if no time had passed.

"Here, let me pour you some wine," Abe said, uncorking a bottle of rich Cabernet Sauvignon with a satisfying pop. He filled their glasses, and they clinked them together in a toast to happy reunions.

"Cheers!" they chorused, sipping the fragrant liquid as it warmed their insides.

A sudden bout of coughing from Lydia interrupted their merriment. Delilah and Abe exchanged concerned glances, but Lydia waved it off with a dismissive hand. "It's just the smoke from those recent fires," she assured them, her voice raspy. "Nothing to worry about."

As dinner came to an end, Delilah excused herself, her thoughts racing ahead to her planned meeting with Jobe. Her heart fluttered with anxiety as she made her way to their rendezvous point, a quaint little coffee shop near the Gozan River.

When Delilah made it to the coffee shop, she was so nervous to see Jobe that her hand trembled as she reached for the door. She opened it and stepped inside.

"Delilah!" Jobe called, waving her over to a secluded corner table. His eyes sparkled with warmth, his smile genuine and inviting. The sight of him sent a jolt through her chest, feelings that had surged since Jobe's recent visit.

"Hey, Jobe!" she greeted him, trying to keep her voice steady. "Thanks for meeting me here."

"Of course!" Jobe stood up and gave her a big hug, and they both sat down and settled into their seats.

"You look great," Jobe told her. "I love the dark hair."

Delilah nearly melted at the compliment because she had been unsure about going brunette since she had gotten her hair dyed. But, as usual, Jobe had said exactly what she needed to hear—and when she needed to hear it.

"Thanks, Jobe," said Delilah with a smile, running a hand through her dark locks. "Yeah, I wasn't sure about it at first—you know I'm used to doing a brighter color."

"That's true," said Jobe. "Red, strawberry blonde, platinum. But this is really nice. It's subdued but elegant." And he looked her in the eyes for a few seconds and smiled slightly.

Delilah met his gaze unflinchingly, and there was so much said between them without words.

"I'll get coffee," said Jobe, rising from his chair and walking to the counter. He returned several minutes later with two coffees.

After catching up excitedly for nearly an hour, Delilah remembered something she needed Jobe's help with. "I wanted to practice my speech for Michelle's wedding, and I could really use your input."

"Of course, I'm happy to help," Jobe replied, leaning back in his chair as Delilah pulled out a crumpled piece of paper from her pocket. She hesitated slightly, then began to recite her speech, her words filled with love and admiration for Michelle.

As she spoke, Jobe listened intently, his gaze never leaving her face. He nodded occasionally, his expression thoughtful and focused. When she finished, he leaned forward, offering his critiques with kindness and sincerity.

"Delilah, that was beautiful," Jobe said, his voice gentle but firm. "But maybe try to add a personal anecdote or two, something that really shows the depth of your friendship with Michelle. It'll make the speech even more heartfelt."

"Thank you, Jobe," Delilah replied, touched by his words. "I appreciate your honest feedback." She looked into his eyes, feeling the connection between them intensify. The unanswered questions about her feelings for Jobe and Jude swirled around her mind, leaving her torn and restless.

Jobe had been a steadying presence in her life, reliable and consistent. It felt like he had always been there for her, and, perhaps, always would. Jude, on the other hand, was ambitious and exciting. There was an unknown aspect about him that drew her in, and undeniable charisma that attracted her.

As they parted ways, Delilah's heart felt heavy with impending decisions. The meeting with Jobe had only served to muddy the waters further, adding fuel to the fire of her emotions. As she made her way back to Abe's house, she wondered what the future held for her relationships, and whether the answers she sought would ever become clear.

THE SUN WAS high in the sky, casting bright hues over the Gozan River as it sparkled behind Michelle and Juan. The air was thick with the perfume of blooming flowers, carried by a gentle breeze that rustled through the leaves of the towering trees that framed the picturesque scene.

Michelle stood at the altar, radiant in her flowing wedding dress. Delicate lace adorned the bodice while the skirt seemed to float around her like a soft cloud. Her dark hair was swept up into an intricate updo, with tendrils softly framing her face. Juan looked dashing in his tailored suit, his floral handkerchief folded stylishly in his front pocket. His eyes were filled with love and admiration for his bride. His black hair was styled impeccably and glistened under the midday sun.

Guests murmured excitedly, their faces beaming with joy as they awaited the ceremony. Delilah couldn't help but feel a wave of emotion wash over her as she watched her lifelong friend prepare to embark on this new chapter of her life. Her grip tightened around the bouquet of flowers in her hand as she thought about the speech she'd give later at the reception. She was nervous but ready.

As the ceremony began, the atmosphere was electric, with the love between Michelle and Juan showing in every word, glance, or gesture. They exchanged heartfelt vows, sealing their commitment with a passionate kiss that drew enthusiastic applause from the crowd.

That evening, the reception unfolded beneath a canopy of twinkling fairy lights, casting a warm glow upon the elegantly set tables. Delilah took center stage, her heart pounding in her chest as she prepared to deliver her speech. She locked eyes with Michelle, who smiled encouragingly, and cleared her throat.

"Michelle, my dearest friend," Delilah began, her voice tinged with emotion. "From the moment we met, I knew our bond was something special. Through laughter and tears, triumphs and obstacles, we've navigated this journey called life side by side."

As she continued, she wove in personal anecdotes, painting a vivid picture of their friendship's depth and resilience. The crowd listened intently, their expressions a mix of amusement and sentimentality.

"Michelle, I am honored to stand beside you on this day as you begin the next chapter with Juan, a man who truly cherishes your beautiful spirit," Delilah concluded, her voice choked with emotion. "May your love continue to grow and flourish, like the majestic trees surrounding us today."

A hush fell over the guests before they erupted into applause, tears glistening in their eyes. Michelle embraced Delilah tightly, her own eyes brimming with grateful tears. As Delilah returned to her seat, she couldn't help but reflect on the power of love and friendship—the strength it held to bind two souls together through all of life's trials.

Delilah could feel the warmth of her cheeks as she stepped away from the applause, the praise and pride swelling within her after delivering the speech. The sun was set-

"Absolutely!" Delilah agreed. "Michelle and Juan look so happy—they deserve all the love in the world."

"Speaking of love," said Jonathan, Jobe's longest and closest friend. He raised his own glass with a sly grin. "I believe we should celebrate that which has brought us all together tonight." Abe and Lydia joined in the toast, their eyes twinkling with shared amusement.

As the night wore on, Delilah found herself drawn to Jobe's side with increasing frequency, their laughter mingling with the din of the joyous reception. They danced, swaying in time to the rhythm as Delilah's thoughts raced, questions swirling like leaves caught in a whirlwind. Was there something more to this connection between them?

"Hey, Delilah," Jobe said softly, his breath warm against her ear. "Want to take a walk with me? Get some fresh air?"

"Sure," she replied, her pulse quickening at the thought of being alone with him.

They slipped away from the festivities, snatching a bottle of champagne from a nearby table as they went. The moon cast a silvery glow upon the riverbank, its surface rippling like liquid mercury under the starry sky. The air was cool and crisp, providing a welcome reprieve from the heated press of bodies on the dance floor.

"Here's to love," Jobe whispered, uncorking the champagne with a satisfying pop. The bubbles fizzed and overflowed, spilling down the sides of the bottle as he handed it to Delilah.

"Love indeed," she murmured, taking a swig of the effervescent liquid. Its taste was sweet and tangy, a perfect counterpoint to the heady rush of emotions surging within her.

As they walked along the riverbank, the world seemed to shrink around them until all that existed was the gentle lapping of the water against the shore and the soft rustle of leaves in the breeze. Delilah felt a magnetic pull toward Jobe, an irresistible force that drew her closer and closer until their fingers intertwined, and their lips met in a passionate kiss that set her soul ablaze.

This was the connection she had yearned for, an unspoken understanding that transcended words and bridged the chasm between two hearts. And yet, uncertainty reared its ugly head once more: what did this mean for her future? For their future?

"Jobe..." she whispered into the darkness as they broke apart, breathless and flushed. "What happens now?"

"Right now, we live in the moment," he replied, his voice husky with emotion. "Tomorrow is a new day."

Delilah nodded, knowing that whatever lay ahead, she would face it with courage and resolve—and perhaps, if fate allowed, with Jobe by her side.

The night air was alive with laughter and music as Delilah and Jobe returned to the reception, their fingers entwined. The glow of the lanterns illuminated Michelle's radiant smile as she danced with her husband, Juan. Delilah felt a surge of warmth in her chest, watching her friend bask in her happiness.

"Congratulations, you two!" Delilah exclaimed, pulling them both into a tight embrace while Jobe stood by, grinning. "You make such a beautiful couple."

"Thank you, Delilah," Michelle beamed, her eyes shining with unshed tears. "Your speech… it meant the world to me."

"Same here," Juan chimed in, his arm wrapped around his bride. "We're lucky to have friends like you."

As they exchanged pleasantries, Delilah couldn't help but steal glances at Jobe, wondering what their stolen kiss might mean for their future. Her heart raced at the thought, yet she knew now was not the time for such contemplations. Instead, she focused on the joyous occasion unfolding around her.

"Michelle, your wedding has been absolutely magical," Delilah said earnestly, her gaze locked onto her friend's. "I'm so grateful to be a part of it."

"Trust me, it wouldn't have been the same without you," Michelle replied, squeezing Delilah's hand before turning to dance with Juan once more.

As the night wore on, the celebration began to wind down, and Michelle and Juan shared one last dance under the moonlit sky. Guests slowly trickled out, leaving behind a trail of discarded plates and half-empty glasses. Delilah found herself standing with her family and close friends, reflecting on the wonderful evening.

"Time flies, doesn't it?" Lydia mused, her eyes misty with emotion. "Feels like just yesterday we were all kids, and now look at us."

"Indeed," Abe agreed, smiling at Lydia. "But it's moments like these that make life worth living."

Abe and Lydia had divorced amicably twelve years ago and had remained on friendly terms. Even though they were no longer married, it warmed Delilah's heart just to see them together.

Jonathan, who had been silently observing the scene, raised an eyebrow. " I couldn't help but notice you and Jobe seemed to have shared some quality alone time by the river."

Delilah's cheeks flushed with heat, and she glanced at Jobe, who returned her gaze with an enigmatic smile. A flutter of nerves danced in her stomach, but she managed to maintain her composure as she replied, "Yes, we did."

"I don't know what happens next," Jobe whispered, leaning in close so that only Delilah could hear him, "but I'm willing to take a chance and find out."

As they stood by the riverbank, watching their friends and family say their goodbyes, Delilah reflected on the whirlwind of emotions that had engulfed her throughout the evening. The love and camaraderie that surrounded her, the passion that had ignited between her and Jobe, and the uncertainty of what lay ahead—each experience had left its indelible mark upon her soul.

The final notes of the band's farewell song reverberated through the air, mingling with the laughter and conversation that filled the night. Delilah, her heart pounding in her chest, stole a glance at Jobe as they stood side by side, watching the guests filter out one by one. The warmth of his presence radiated against her skin, stirring a longing within her that defied explanation.

"Isn't it strange," she mused aloud, "how a single event can change everything you thought you knew about yourself?"

Jobe looked over at her, his eyes alight with curiosity. "What do you mean?"

Delilah hesitated, her gaze drifting to the flickering candles that lined the path. "I guess I never truly understood how much I wanted…this." She gestured vaguely at the scene before them. "A partner, someone to share my life with."

"Is that so?" Jobe asked, his voice barely more than a whisper. He leaned closer, his breath warm on her cheek. "Tell me, Delilah—have you found that person yet?"

A shiver ran down her spine, and she met his gaze, her eyes searching for something she couldn't quite define. "I think I might have," she admitted, her pulse quickening. "But I'm not sure if he feels the same way."

Jobe smiled at her and took her hand.

Their fingers intertwined, and they followed the candlelit path away from the reception area, stealing furtive glances at each other as they walked. The rustle of leaves beneath their feet seemed to echo the tumultuous emotions that swirled between them, threatening to consume them both.

"Jobe," Delilah began, her voice wavering slightly, "I need to know. Do you…feel the same way about me?"

The intensity of his gaze made her tremble as he searched her face for a moment, seeming to be weighing his words. "Delilah," he said finally, his voice low and charged. "As I see you so clearly again tonight, I know there is something between us. It terrifies me, but at the same time, I can't deny it."

"Neither can I," she whispered, her heart pounding in her chest.

"I can't lie to myself anymore," Jobe said, his grip on her hand tightening. "I know how I feel about you—how I've always felt."

With that, he pulled her close, their lips meeting in a passionate kiss that seemed to burn away everything that had come before. As they broke apart, Delilah felt a newfound sense of purpose taking root inside her—a certainty that no matter what lay ahead, she knew Jobe felt the same way as her.

But as she thought about the bottle of champagne they had shared, she wondered if it was the alcohol that had made them both so honest. Tomorrow, in the harsh light of day, would they both be willing to say the same things?

CHAPTER THIRTEEN

Knowing she would be flying back to New York, was there even a point to them doing so?

She didn't know. What she did know was that having Jobe so close just felt right. So right.

They left the wedding, hand in hand.

While Jobe offered to walk her home, Delilah was enjoying Jobe's company far too much. She didn't want the night to end.

"I want to go with you," she said as she gazed into his eyes. They headed to Jobe's house and opened a bottle of wine.

CHAPTER FOURTEEN

Delilah's heels clicked against the pavement as she walked down the bustling New York streets, her mind a whirlwind of memories from Michelle's wedding. Her heart swelled with happiness, recalling the joyous celebration and the time spent reuniting with friends and family. Though underneath it all, a deep ache settled in her chest as she felt herself missing someone—Jobe. The thought of him ignited a fire within her, but she was frustrated by the distance that separated them.

As she stepped into her office building, Delilah tried to shake off the despair that threatened to consume her. She couldn't fathom the possibility that she and Jobe would never live in the same place long enough for anything lasting to happen between them. It seemed like a cruel joke, as if fate was playing with her emotions.

"Hey, Delilah!" Jenia greeted her as she approached her desk, snapping her out of her thoughts. "How was the wedding?"

"Amazing," Delilah replied, forcing a smile onto her face. "It was great seeing everyone again."

"Speaking of seeing people," Jenia said, wiggling her eyebrows playfully, "I've got some news of my own. I'm dating this fantastic new guy!"

"Really?" Delilah asked, feigning excitement while her heart sank deeper into loneliness. "Tell me more."

"His name's Alex, and he's just incredible," Jenia gushed, her eyes sparkling with enthusiasm.

We met at this art gallery a couple of weeks ago, and we've been inseparable ever since."

While Delilah listened to Jenia's story, she couldn't help but feel a hollow emptiness gnawing at her. Sure, she had her dream job and a comfortable salary, but it all felt meaningless without a partner to share it with.

"Congratulations, Jenia. He sounds wonderful," Delilah said, the words leaving a bitter taste in her mouth.

"Thanks! We're going out tonight. Maybe next time you can join us. You never know who you might meet," Jenia suggested with a wink.

"Maybe," Delilah replied noncommittally, knowing full well that she would rather spend the evening wallowing in her thoughts of Jobe and what could have been.

As the day wore on, Delilah struggled to focus on her work. Her mind kept drifting back to Michelle's wedding and the intoxicating connection she had shared with Jobe. If only they could be together, maybe the emptiness threatening to swallow her whole would dissipate.

CHAPTER FOURTEEN

But as the sun began to set and the city lights flickered to life, Delilah knew she couldn't keep dwelling on the what-ifs. She had to face the reality of her situation—Jobe was far away, and there was no guarantee that their paths would ever cross again. And yet, the thought of letting him go was too painful to bear.

"Delilah, are you okay?" Jenia asked, noticing her friend's distant expression as they left the office.

"I'm fine," Delilah lied, forcing another smile. "Just a little tired."

"Get some rest, okay? We'll catch up tomorrow."

"Thanks, Jenia," Delilah replied, watching her coworker walk away before turning toward her car.

Alone in her apartment, Delilah poured herself a glass of wine and sank into her favorite armchair. As she stared out at the twinkling cityscape, she couldn't help but ponder her future, wondering when—or if—her time for love would ever come.

The next day at work, Delilah found herself unable to concentrate on her tasks. Her mind was occupied with thoughts of love and the possibility of finding someone who could fill the void in her heart. As she stared blankly at her notebook, Jenia approached her desk.

"Hey, Delilah," Jenia said with a mischievous smile, leaning against the edge of the desk. "I've been thinking…I know a great guy for you. What do you say? Are you up for a blind date?"

Delilah hesitated, her thoughts instantly drifting to Jobe, and even her complicated emotions surrounding Jude. Jobe—the man who really saw her for who she was and would always accept her. And Jude—the charismatic and commanding presence who challenged her. The idea of adding another person to the mix seemed overwhelming. But at the same time, she couldn't deny that she longed for companionship and love.

"Jenia, I appreciate it, but I'm not sure if I'm ready for something like that right now. My life's a bit…chaotic," Delilah admitted, her eyes darting away from Jenia's hopeful expression.

"Trust me, this guy is wonderful. He's my cousin's friend, and he's charming, successful, and kind. I think you two would hit it off," Jenia insisted, placing a comforting hand on Delilah's shoulder.

"Maybe…. Just give me some time to think about it, okay?" Delilah replied, torn between wanting to take a chance at happiness and fearing the consequences of diving headfirst into another emotional entanglement.

"Of course, take all the time you need. But remember, life is short, and sometimes we need to take a leap of faith," Jenia said warmly, giving Delilah's shoulder a reassuring squeeze before walking away.

As the workday came to an end, Delilah couldn't shake the feeling of loneliness and despair that weighed heavy on her chest. She drove home lost in thought, her mind a whirlwind of conflicting emotions.

Delilah sank into her armchair and stared out at the city lights. She thought of Jobe, the undeniable chemistry between them, and the distance that separated their lives. She thought of Jude, his ambition and cunning nature, and how he had challenged her in ways she never imagined. And now, the possibility of meeting someone loomed on the horizon, adding another layer of complexity to her already tumultuous love life.

"Is it worth the risk?" Delilah whispered to herself, her heart aching for something she couldn't quite grasp.

As she sat there, contemplating her future and the choices that lay before her, Delilah couldn't help but wonder if true love was something that would ever find its way into her life—or if it was merely a fleeting dream, destined to remain just out of reach.

LYDIA'S PEN DANCED over her notebook, the gliding of the pen a soothing backdrop to the memories swirling in her mind. She smiled as she recalled the joyful atmosphere of Michelle's wedding. Seeing Abe, Jobe, and Michelle— now happily married to Juan—had filled her with warmth and nostalgia.

"Is everything okay, Lydia?" a coworker inquired, noticing her smile.

"Everything's more than okay," she replied, her eyes sparkling with genuine happiness. "I was just thinking about my friend's wedding I attended recently."

"Ah, weddings always have that magical touch, don't they?"

"Indeed," she agreed, her thoughts drifting back to the celebration.

The memory of the wedding served as a stark contrast to the dangers she had faced during the arson investigation and her confrontation with Luke Belial. As she sat at her desk, she marveled at how much more capable she felt after those harrowing experiences. Graduating college, landing her dream job, and tackling that dangerous assignment had all contributed to her personal growth, and she reveled in this newfound sense of accomplishment.

"Lydia, could you take a look at these reports for me?" her boss asked, pulling her from her reverie.

"Of course," she responded, immersing herself in the task at hand. Her analytical mind dissected every detail, ensuring its accuracy.

As Lydia tackled the challenges before her, she couldn't help but think of Delilah. Her daughter had been through so much turmoil recently, particularly when it came to her love life. Lydia wished she could give guidance or support, but she knew Delilah needed to find her own path.

CHAPTER FOURTEEN

Mom, what do I do? Delilah's voice echoed in her head, a memory from a recent conversation. *Jobe and Jude are both amazing, but they're so different—and I don't know if I can handle another person in the mix.*

"Sometimes our hearts must guide us, even when our minds are uncertain," she had told her daughter, hoping her words would bring some comfort.

As Lydia finished reviewing the financial reports, she glanced at the clock, realizing the workday was drawing to an end. With a sense of purpose, she gathered her belongings and prepared to head home, eager to spend the evening reflecting on her journey and the lessons she had learned along the way. She couldn't help but wonder what challenges awaited her— and her cherished daughter—in the days to come.

Lydia stood up from her desk, a determined glint in her eyes. The sun was setting, casting golden rays across the cityscape outside her window. As she gazed upon the bustling streets below, her eyes fell on a familiar sight: the Phoenix truck. The mythical creature painted on its side seemed to leap out at her, wings spread wide as if taking flight.

Look at that, she thought, heart swelling with pride, I've soared to new heights, haven't I?

She grabbed her coat and purse, and in a flurry of determination, strode out of the office. Her heels clicked rhythmically against the floor, echoing through the empty corridors. She couldn't wait to get home and unwind, allowing herself a moment of respite from the challenges that had defined her recent days.

"Good evening, Lydia!" the security guard called as she passed by his post. She offered a warm smile in return, acknowledging his friendly presence.

"Good evening, Tom. Have a great night!"

Once outside, the cool air nipped at her cheeks as she hurried toward her car. The streets were alive with the hum of traffic and pedestrians rushing to their various destinations. At that moment, Lydia felt invigorated, her spirit soaring alongside the painted Phoenix that had captivated her attention just moments before.

Upon arriving home, she wasted no time in shedding her work attire and slipping into something more comfortable. Her hand reached for a bottle of wine, the glass clinking gently against the counter as she poured herself a generous serving. She carried the wine to the living room, sinking into the plush cushions of her couch with a contented sigh.

"Delilah," she murmured, concern flickering across her features. "That girl's been through so much lately."

As she sipped her wine, Lydia's thoughts drifted to her daughter—brave, resilient Delilah. She couldn't help but worry about her, even as she recognized that Delilah needed to forge her own path.

She'll figure it out, Lydia mused, a proud smile tugging at her lips. Just like her mother.

The room was filled with a comfortable silence, broken only by the occasional chime of Lydia's glass against the table as she took another sip. Her mind wandered to the arson ordeal, the memories of taking down Luke Belial still vivid and fresh. It had been a harrowing experience, one that had tested her resolve and forced her to confront her fears. But in the end, she had emerged victorious, stronger than ever before.

"I've learned so much," she whispered into the quiet, the words barely more than a breath. "And I'm sure there are more lessons yet to come."

Lydia drained the last of her wine and set the empty glass aside. As she rose from the couch, she caught a glimpse of her reflection in the window. The woman who stared back at her was one of strength, determination, and unyielding spirit—a woman who refused to be held down by adversity.

Here's to new heights, she thought with a grin.

With that, Lydia retreated to her bedroom. Sleep came easily that night, her dreams filled with images of the mighty Phoenix taking wing, guiding both her and Delilah toward their destinies.

IN THE DIM, flickering light of her apartment, Delilah stared into her wine glass, swirling the rich red liquid and watching it cling to the sides. She had always found solace in these quiet moments, a reprieve from the chaos of her life. But tonight, the solitude felt heavy, oppressive even—like an ever-tightening vice around her heart. With a sigh, she took a long sip, allowing the warmth of the wine to spread through her chest and loosen the knots that had formed there.

"Jobe," she whispered, his name tasting bittersweet on her tongue. She missed him terribly—the way he made her laugh, the comforting strength of his arms around her. But the distance between them seemed insurmountable, a chasm that grew wider with each passing day. Would they ever find a way to bridge that gap? Or were they destined to be star-crossed lovers, never quite able to reach one another?

As she continued to drink, her thoughts turned inward, picking at old wounds and lingering fears. If she could not be with Jobe, was she somehow unworthy of love? Did her wanderlust and desire for adventure make her unlovable? The questions swirled around her like a tempest, threatening to swallow her whole.

I just want to be with someone who understands me, who loves me despite my flaws, she thought, tears pricking at the corners of her eyes. *Is that too much to ask?*

Suddenly, the quiet was broken by a soft knock on the door, jolting Delilah from her melancholy musings. She froze in place, her heart thumping wildly in her chest as she stared at the wooden barrier before her. Who could be on the other side?

The anticipation settled around her like a fog, prickling across her skin and filling every corner of her being with wonder and excitement. She held her breath for a moment before finally mustering up the courage to stand and answer.

Delilah took a deep breath. "Who is it?"

"It's me, Jude!" called a voice from outside her door, pulling her abruptly from her melancholy reverie.

As she swung open the door, her eyes widened in surprise. There stood Jude, his normally confident demeanor replaced by raw vulnerability. His gaze met hers, and for a moment, time seemed to freeze.

Delilah felt a mix of emotions coursing through her as she stared into Jude's eyes. Nervousness bubbled up in her stomach, yet the air around them seemed to shimmer with both desire and confusion. She was suddenly overwhelmed with longing, wishing that he would somehow understand all the words that she could not bring herself to say. Yet despite the turmoil in her heart, one thought remained constant—that perhaps this was the start of something new.

"Can I come in?" he asked her. The weight of that question hung in the air between them, laden with unspoken emotions and unsaid words.

It was midnight, and she'd had quite a bit to drink— letting Jude in now was not a smart thing to do. Delilah hesitated for a moment, but her inhibitions had melted away with the last drops of wine. She felt a sense of warmth and familiarity, and she found herself smiling, feeling as if something long dormant had been stirred awake—something that had been missing from her life for the last several months.

"Sure. I'll pour you a glass of wine."

Thoughts swarmed Delilah's mind as they sat side by side on the couch. There were so many feelings regarding Jude—fear, attraction, distrust, desire—and it was not easy to know what to do with him sitting right next to her, his hand rubbing softly across the top of her bare thigh.

And while she was uncertain of what path to take, Jude certainly wasn't, for he had now leaned in to kiss her neck, his hands tugging on the straps of her nightgown.

Perhaps she will let her uncertainty drift away.

CHAPTER FIFTEEN

Jobe stood on the stage, his heart pounding like a drum. The school's auditorium was packed with students, parents, and faculty, all gathered for the annual awards ceremony. As he accepted the commendation for his exceptional teaching, his face flushed with pride. He could feel the hive-like bumps forming on his skin, an inevitable side effect of his stress and excitement.

"Thank you," he said, his voice steady despite the adrenaline coursing through him. "I couldn't have done this without the support of my incredible students, colleagues, and friends."

The applause was deafening, and as he stepped down from the stage, Jobe felt a sense of fulfillment that he had never experienced before.

Later that evening, Jobe returned to his quiet home, his golden retriever, Smokey, jumping on him excitedly when he arrived. A gentle rain had fallen while he was gone, leaving the world outside damp and glistening. As he stepped into his backyard, he noticed a tiny seed sprouting from the soil, its delicate green leaves reaching for the sky.

Delilah would love this, he thought, remembering the tree they had planted near the church in Mount Moriah. At that moment, he decided to pay it a visit, hoping the sight of their shared labor would bring them closer, even if only in spirit.

Jobe climbed into his car, the engine roaring to life beneath him. As he sped toward the church, his thoughts were consumed by Delilah—her warmth, her laughter, and the memories they had made.

He approached the church, the building that his father had started—and Jobe had finished. In that sacred space, he and Delilah had buried their own seed of hope, a symbol of their shared dreams and desires.

As Jobe stepped out onto the church grounds, his eyes fell upon the tree. It was still young and growing tall, standing about twelve feet from the ground. Its branches stretched toward the heavens like outstretched arms. In its shadow, he could almost feel the presence of his father and the love he had shared with Delilah.

"Look at what we've done," he whispered, placing a hand on the tree's smooth bark. "You're here with me, even when you're not."

For a moment, Jobe stood there, lost in thought. He wondered what Delilah would think if she saw their tree now—how it had flourished, just as their friendship had.

Jobe took one last look around—at the churchyard, the church itself, and at the tree. A new chapter was beginning, and he was excited for what was to come.

LYDIA WROTE IN her notebook, weaving data and insights into a powerful report. The hum of her coworkers' hushed conversations filled the office, a dynamic symphony punctuated by the rustling of papers around her. In this energetic atmosphere, Lydia thrived, her keen mind working in perfect harmony with her diligent work ethic.

"Excuse me, Lydia?" someone called from behind her.

Startled, she turned to find Rico standing at her desk. His serious presence loomed like an unexpected storm cloud, but his warm smile dispelled any tension.

"Could I have a word with you in my office, please?" he asked, gesturing toward the glass-walled room that overlooked the open workspace.

"Of course," she replied, curiosity piquing as she followed him inside.

Rico closed the door behind them, shutting out the ambient noise and creating an intimate cocoon. He leaned against his desk, hands clasped, and looked at Lydia intently. "Lydia, I wanted to personally commend your exceptional work since joining our team. Your attention to detail and analytical prowess have proven invaluable," he said, his words carrying genuine appreciation. "Not to mention your bravery in dealing with the arsonist. And for that, we're giving you a one-week paid vacation so you can decompress from everything." Rico winked. "And we're covering your airfare, too. In the event you don't want to take a trip, and you want to have a 'staycation' instead, your flight voucher will be good for whenever you'd like to use it."

Lydia gasped. "Wow, Rico. Thank you so much! I'm grateful for the opportunity to put my skills to good use," she responded, feeling a swell of pride and appreciation.

"Your ability to build meaningful relationships with your coworkers has not gone unnoticed either. It's clear that they respect and value your contributions, both professionally and personally."

Lydia's thoughts wandered briefly to Delilah, recalling the strength of their bond and the support they supplied each other. She hoped that her daughter was experiencing the same level of connection in her own life. "Thanks again, Rico. I believe that we can achieve great things when we work together," Lydia replied.

"I couldn't agree more," Rico said, nodding. "Keep up the outstanding work, Lydia. You're an essential part of this team."

As Lydia left Rico's office, she felt a sense of accomplishment radiating through her veins. She had faced countless challenges throughout her life, and she was proud of the person she had become—strong, compassionate, and driven to make a difference in the world.

Lydia strode through the bustling office, pausing to exchange a few words with her colleagues. A warm laugh from Anna as they discussed their shared love for hiking, an enthusiastic handshake with Sam over their recent project success, and a quick check-in with Carmen about her daughter's piano recital—these small moments wove the tapestry of relationships she had built at work.

"Great job on that presentation this morning, Lydia!" called out Carlos, giving her a thumbs-up from his desk.

"Thanks, Carlos," she replied with a smile. "Couldn't have done it without your input."

As Lydia wrapped up her day, she felt a genuine sense of camaraderie with her team. These connections had become an essential part of her life, providing not only professional support but also a source of friendship and belonging.

She hurried home, eager to continue reflecting on her journey. As soon as she stepped inside, she kicked off her shoes, poured herself a glass of red wine, and settled into her favorite armchair. Sipping the rich, velvety liquid, Lydia allowed her mind to wander—back to the challenges she had faced, the people who had walked alongside her, and the lessons life had taught her.

Michelle's comforting presence came to mind, her friendship a guiding light for both her and Delilah.

Lydia was grateful for Michelle's empathy, wisdom, and gentle encouragement.

And then there was Delilah, her amazing daughter. Memories of Delilah flashed before Lydia's eyes—teaching her how to ride a bike, watching her graduate, seeing her take flight in her career. Lydia's heart swelled with pride and love.

The evening sun cast a warm glow across the room, and Lydia closed her eyes and allowed herself to bask in the contentment that filled her soul. She knew life would continue to throw challenges their way, but with her loved ones by her side, she was ready to face whatever came next.

And later, as the darkness settled around her, somewhere deep within, Lydia felt the stirrings of a new chapter beginning—one filled with uncertainty, adventure, and the promise of growth. But for now, she simply breathed in the peace that surrounded her, knowing that she had everything she needed right there, in the arms of those she loved most.

"HEY, DELILAH! NEED any help with that presentation?" called out Jenia, her friendly coworker who always seemed willing to help.

"Thanks, but I've got it under control!" she responded with a grin, feeling grateful for the relationships she had built in this new environment.

"All right. Let me know if you change your mind," he said, giving her a thumbs-up before turning back to his own work.

Delilah continued to excel in her job, driving key projects forward and collaborating effortlessly with her colleagues. It was clear to everyone around her that she was thriving here, her natural charisma and communication skills making her a magnet for success.

Finally, the clock struck five, and Delilah put her work away, and waved goodbye to her coworkers as she exited the building. Slipping into her car, she reflected on the whirlwind journey she had been on recently. Starting this job, being maid of honor at Michelle's wedding, and seeing both Jobe and Jude in unexpected circumstances.

"Life certainly doesn't let up, does it?" she mused aloud, navigating the busy streets with practiced ease.

Memories of the wedding flashed in her mind—Michelle in her stunning gown, the heartfelt speeches, and the laughter shared by all. She smiled, feeling a warm glow spread through her chest at the thought of her dear friend's happiness.

But mingled with the joy were moments of confusion and concern—thoughts of Jobe and Jude that left her questioning her own actions, her own feelings and her own priorities. What did their presence in her life signify? And what path should she choose moving forward?

These questions swirled around her head, but Delilah pushed them away again, determined to focus on the beauty that life had brought her recently.

As she drove home, she caught sight of the mural that her mother had commissioned to be painted on the Nod Warehouse. A phoenix rising from the ashes, its fiery red wings spread out majestically as it flew into a new day. Delilah felt a wave of warmth wash over her at the sight of it—a reminder of resilience and hope in times of difficulty. The intricate details were breathtakingly beautiful, feathers composed of stunning scarlets and oranges that danced in the light, each one crafted with care and precision. A crown adorned its head, glimmering with golden accents as if to symbolize inner strength and courage even amid chaos. Finally, two powerful eyes stared ahead boldly—urging all who saw it to never give up no matter what their circumstances may be.

It was a breathtaking sight, one that seemed to hold a promise of hope and new beginnings.

The road stretched out before her, seemingly endless, and as she pressed her foot down on the accelerator, she felt a surge of excitement and anticipation. There were so many possibilities in life, and she wondered where her next adventure would take her. *There's only one way to find out.*

And with that, Delilah Boaz raced toward her future, her heart filled with an unshakable belief in herself and the promise of growth that lay just beyond the horizon.

DELILAH'S HANDS SHOOK as she fumbled with the small white box in her hands, her fingers nearly ripping through the cheap cardboard. The bathroom light hummed above, casting a harsh glow on the sterile tiles that lined the floor and walls.

"Okay, Delilah, just breathe," she whispered to herself, her eyes flickering to the instructions printed on the side of the pregnancy test. "Two lines means pregnant…one line means not."

Her pulse throbbed in her ears as she tore open the foil wrapper, revealing the plastic stick inside. She braced herself for what might come next and followed the instructions, waiting with bated breath as the test began to process.

Her palms moistened, her mind racing as she tried to imagine the implications of the test result. Would this change everything? How would it affect her relationships with Jobe, Jude, and everyone else in her life?

She stared at the small window on the test where the results would appear. Time seemed to slow down, each second stretching into an eternity as her heartbeat echoed throughout the room.

And then, suddenly, two pink lines appeared, clear as day.

"Positive," Delilah said, her heart skipping a beat as the news settled onto her shoulders. She closed her eyes, trying to wrap her head around the enormity of what this meant.

Delilah trembled as a whirlwind of emotions swirled within her.

Make it be so.

Path Talk

Bald Solomon: During Path Talk, I usually talk directly with a character, asking a variety of questions to get an insightful conversation going. However, not this time. Delilah just found out she is pregnant, and I merely need to listen. Here she is…

Delilah: Shock. Total, utter shock. How is this even possible? I didn't plan for this, not now. My heart's pounding so loud, I can barely hear my own thoughts. This can't be real, can it? But it is, it's happening to me. To me, Delilah.

What am I going to do? The father… what will he say? He's not ready—I'm not ready. We're not even… we're not even stable. How can I bring a child into this? A baby, a real, living baby. My baby.

Mom and Dad, oh my goodness, Mom and Dad. They're going to be so disappointed, or worried, or both. They have such high hopes for me. This will change everything. Will they support me? They have to, right? They're my parents. But what if they don't? What if they turn away from me?

And my friends, my job, my life… it's all going to change. Everything's going to change. I'm scared. So scared. But wait, there's a life inside me. A tiny, innocent life. That's…

incredible. Terrifying, but incredible. I'm going to be a mother. Me, a mother. Can I do this? Can I really do this?

I need to breathe, just breathe. I can handle this, right? I'm strong, I've always been strong. But this is different; this is huge. I need help. I can't do this alone. I have to tell someone. I need to make a plan, a real plan.

But first, I need to accept this, accept that I'm going to be a mom. My whole world is about to change, and... maybe that's not a bad thing? Maybe this is a new path, a new journey for me. Scary, unexpected, but maybe... maybe it could be wonderful?

Okay, Delilah, focus. You've always faced challenges head-on. This... this is just another challenge, right? A huge one, but still. Breathe. You've got this. You have to have this.

My job, my career – how will I manage? I've always been ambitious, driven. A baby changes everything. Can I still chase my dreams, or do they change now too? And the travel, the freedom I cherished – how much of that am I giving up?

But wait, I'm not alone in this. There are other single moms out there, right? Capable women who handle this kind of thing every day. I can learn from them, lean on them for support. I'm part of a new community now.

And my baby, my child. What will they be like? Will they have my eyes, my laugh? What dreams will they chase? What joys will they find in life? I get to see all that and be part of it. That's... that's pretty incredible.

But J**e... How do I even begin that conversation? What if he doesn't want this? What if he does? Are we going to co-parent, or am I on my own? This conversation is going to be one of the hardest I've ever had.

I need to make some decisions, big ones. About where I live, about my health, about the future. It's overwhelming. This is real, and it's happening.

There's strength in me, I know it. I've always relied on it. It's just being tested in a way I never expected. But maybe... maybe I can do this. Maybe I can be a great mom. Maybe this unexpected journey is exactly what I need. Scary, but maybe also a blessing?

J**e. How do I even approach him? It's like standing at the edge of a cliff, knowing I have to jump but not knowing what awaits below. This isn't just any conversation, it's one that could change everything. Again.

What will I see on his face when I tell him? Will it be shock, anger, or something else? I can't predict his reaction, and that's terrifying. We didn't plan for this. We are still like two ships passing in the night, and now, suddenly, we're tethered by this unforeseen circumstance.

I rehearse the words in my mind, but they all sound hollow, inadequate. 'I'm pregnant, and you're the father.' How do you casually drop a bombshell like that? It's not just news; it's a life-changer, a responsibility, a tie that will bind us, willingly or not, for the rest of our lives.

And then, what? Do we try to make this work, for the baby's sake? Do I even want that? Can two people thrown together by this create a happy ending? Or is it better to prepare for doing this alone, to brace myself for solo parenthood?

He has a right to know, that much is clear. But rights aside, there's also his potential role in this child's life. What if he wants to be involved? What if he doesn't? Am I ready to co-parent with him, to navigate this complex dynamic for years to come?

This is about more than just him and me now. It's about a new life, an innocent life that deserves the best we can give. We owe it to this child to at least try, to have the conversation, to see what's possible.

Breathe, Delilah. It's time to face the music.

Dad. How do I even start this conversation? Telling him feels like I'm about to walk into a storm. He's always had such high hopes for me, and this... I can't even imagine how he'll take it. He sees the world in black and white, and this is a shade of gray he might not be ready to understand.

He's protective, always has been. But this isn't something he can shield me from. It's real, it's happening, and I'm the one in the middle of it. How do I tell the man who's been my rock that his daughter is pregnant, and it's not a happily-ever-after story?

I can picture his disappointment, his worry. He might feel like he's failed me somehow, or that I've let him down. The weight of that, the thought of adding any burden to him, it's almost too much to bear. But keeping this a secret isn't an option. He needs to know, and I need him now more than ever.

I expect questions, a lot of them. Questions I don't have all the answers to. He'll want to know about the father, about my plans, about what this means for my future. And I'll have to stand there, in front of him, vulnerable and exposed, trying to piece together answers that even I continue to search for.

But there's a part of me, a small part, that hopes for his understanding, for his unconditional love to see us through this. Maybe, just maybe, he'll see past the situation, past the shock and the initial disappointment, and just see me, his daughter, needing his support.

He might surprise me. Dad's always been full of surprises. Beneath that stern exterior is a heart that cares deeply. Maybe he'll be the anchor I need in this chaos. Maybe he'll be the one to help me navigate these uncharted waters.

PATH TALK

But first, I have to tell him. And that's the hardest step. Finding the right words, the right moment, to reveal a truth that will change our lives forever. I just hope that, when all is said and done, we can stand together like we always have, as father and daughter, ready to face whatever comes next.

Okay, Delilah. It's time to be brave. It's time to tell Dad.

Mom. This is going to be so hard. She's been the one I've turned to, the one who understood me when no one else did. But this... How do I tell her I'm pregnant—and in such complicated circumstances?

Mom's always been about strength and independence, about carving your own path. But this feels like I'm veering off the path she hoped I'd follow. She's been my role model, my guide. Will she see this as a mistake, a misstep in my journey?

I can almost hear her voice, trying to process the news, mixed with concern and love. She might be scared for me, scared of the challenges I'll face. I hate the thought of causing her worry, of adding any stress to her life.

Yet, there's a part of me that knows, deep down, that she'll be there for me. She's always had this incredible capacity to embrace life's messiness, to find the silver lining. Maybe she'll help me see this through a different lens, and help me find the strength to handle this.

I know she'll have questions about the father, about my plans for my future. She's pragmatic that way, always looking at the practical side of things. I need to be ready for that, ready to discuss things that I haven't yet figured out myself.

But more than anything, I need her. I need her guidance, her wisdom, her unconditional love. I need to hear her tell me that it's going to be okay, even if we both know it won't be easy.

Mom deserves to know, and I need her by my side.

So, here goes. Time to have the conversation. Time to tell my mom that she's going to be a grandmother. And hope that, no matter what, she'll still see me, her daughter, who needs her now more than ever. It is time to tell Mom.

Life is throwing me a curveball, the biggest one yet. But I've got to step up to the plate. For me, for my baby. We're in this together now. It's a new chapter, a new story to write. My story. Our story. And it starts now. Wow.

Bald Solomon: Delilah, thank you for allowing me to listen in. I understand the tough situation that I wrote into your life story.

The Path Series™ are stories that not only entertain but also resonate deeply with life's realities. You may not fully appreciate this today, but your situation is particularly impactful to the Path Series™. Your journey reflects the voyage we all take through life's twists and turns. At some point, we all face crossroads, much like the one you're at now.

Delilah: I'm listening. Crossroads... that's exactly where I am. Sometimes I just feel so lost in the details that are swirling around in my life. But can a book really help with real-life decisions?

Bald Solomon: Your story, your emotions, your actions, embody the challenges, dilemmas, and triumphs that we all encounter. Through your narrative, the Path Series™ offers guidance, hope, and a sense of connection. You, Delilah, facing your unexpected pregnancy and complex relationships, can be a mirror to our readers, reflecting your experiences and emotions onto their own.

Delilah: A mirror to my life... I can see how that might be helpful.

Bald Solomon: Exactly. And more than that, the Path Series™ provides examples of resilience and courage in the face of adversity. It's about finding strength within oneself, navigating through uncertainty, and making choices that lead to growth and fulfillment.

Delilah: Resilience and courage... I could use some of that right now.

Bald Solomon: That's the spirit. In your journey, you'll find inner resources you didn't know you had. Even better, the Path Series™ can inspire and empower its readers to face their challenges head-on, to seek out their path, even when it seems clouded.

Delilah: It's comforting to know that others have walked similar paths and found their way.

Bald Solomon: Precisely. And remember, every story in the Path Series™ is a testament to the human spirit's ability to overcome and evolve. Your story, too, can be one of transformation and hope.

Delilah: Thank you. Knowing that gives me a bit more courage to face what's ahead.

Bald Solomon: Of course. Thank you for letting us into your world.

Bald Solomon: Please allow me to change perspective and address our readers directly.

As we conclude this edition of Path Talk, I invite you to extend our interactions beyond these pages.

I ask you to share a customer review on Amazon. If you offer a glimpse into your journey or share what resonated with you, you may help guide a new reader to find similar inspiration.

Each thought, each insight you contribute, weaves into the tapestry of shared experiences to enrich our collective understanding of the Path Series™ and our human experience. I need your help to bring this to more people.

Customer Reviews on Amazon are our public square. Please make it be so.

Thank you.

Bald Solomon

Sequel

Path Series™ Book 10
Path Enriched: Embracing Your First Child

"I'm pregnant."

Learn who the father really is. And how he responds.

Delilah Boaz's world spirals into uncertainty and complex emotions. Facing her unplanned pregnancy, she navigates a tumultuous mix of fear, hope, and life-altering decisions.

Amidst her turmoil, Jobe and Jude embark on a life-saving quest through Mexico City for a mystical herb, racing against time and unknown forces.

This riveting tale paints love, resilience, and the pursuit of hope onto a canvas of modern challenges and traditional wisdom. Paths intertwine, blending current struggles with ancient secrets.

Path Enriched is not only an exciting story. It is an adventure of the heart.

Bald Solomon extends our Path Series™ with this lore of intrigue and personal growth, highlighting the force of family love.

MAKE IT BE SO

A Previous Book

Path Series™ Book 6
Path Divided: Surviving Divorce

Go back in time twelve years, to a time when Lydia says is "the most scared I have ever been." Find out what really happened.

Plunge into the impending chaos that is the marriage of Abe and Lydia Boaz. Their once-storybook union teeters on the brink.

Lydia flees to a fresh start in New York, only to be ensnared by a faceless stalker who creates a nightmarish world of fear and paranoia. As the suspense escalates, the enigmatic stalker expands his sights onto Delilah, even while remaining ever elusive.

Dive into the characters' innermost fears and vulnerabilities as they evolve and grow as a newly divided family.

Bald Solomon delivers another fast-moving Path Series™ journey of transformation, resilience, and unbreakable bonds.

Vantage Point

Here are some points to ponder as you start your new job.

Stay Positive. Connect and Communicate. Value Your Work.

Stay Positive

1. In what ways can my positive attitude ease my transition into this new environment?

2. How can I view job challenges as opportunities for personal growth?

3. What actions can I take to make a positive impact from day one?

4. How can I maintain positivity in all my workplace communications?

5. What is the best way to embrace feedback with a positive mindset?

6. Which early achievements should I celebrate?

Connect and Communicate

1. What strategies can I use to create strong bonds with my new colleagues?

2. How can I effectively integrate into the team's existing dynamics?

3. Who are potential mentors in my new workplace?

4. What are the most effective methods for sharing my ideas in team settings?

5. How often should I check in with colleagues to maintain open communication?

Value Your Work

1. What realistic goals can I set to excel in my initial months?

2. In what ways can I add value to my team and company?

3. What steps can I take to ensure top-quality work and consistent excellence?

4. How can my work align with the company's overall objectives?

5. What action can I take now to demonstrate my commitment to my role?

6. How can I get feedback to improve my performance?

Terminus

"You must do the thing you think you cannot do."

—ELEANOR ROOSEVELT.